MW00720897

THE

SOURCE

[Finding Your Way Home]

A continuing saga into the
everlasting life of
Marcus, a Dharmacist, and his Friends…
within and beyond the
"Three Dimensional Earth Plane"…

ISBN 0-7414-2633-1

Copy Editor, Layout & Formatting: Suzanne Strawser Slingbaum, Tampa, Florida

Artwork: Cover Design and Illustrations: Suzanne Strawser Slingbaum, Tampa, Florida

Credit: Planetary Nebula NGC 3132, Hubble Heritage Team (STScI/AURA/NASA)

Surrealistic Painting of the Author's "Eyes" on the Back Cover: Peter Wade, Key West, Florida

Published by:

INFI∞ITY
PUBLISHING.COM

1094 New DeHaven Street, Suite 100
West Conshohocken, PA 19428-2713
Info@buybooksontheweb.com
www.buybooksontheweb.com
Toll-free (877) BUY BOOK
Local Phone (610) 941-9999
Fax (610) 941-9959

Printed in the United States of America
Printed on Recycled Paper
Published July 2005

Special thanks to Suzi; whose dedication and devotion to "Another Place In Space" and "The Source" helped make both books a reality.

Edward Namerdy, who still resides in Key West, began writing this sequel "The Source", in April of 2004. He continues to travel the spiritual path to enlightenment through his writings. Come join him as you experience "The Source – Finding Your Way Home".

A NOTE FROM THE AUTHOR

For those of you that have not read ANOTHER PLACE IN SPACE, of which this book, THE SOURCE, is a sequel to; here is an encapsulation to aid in bringing you up to step.

It is, however, highly recommended that you read ANOTHER PLACE IN SPACE before reading THE SOURCE, although it is not imperative.

In the event that you are already familiar with some basic principles and/or concepts of metaphysics, the following depiction may be adequate enough without your having read ANOTHER PLACE IN SPACE [affectionately called "APIS"].

However, it is my innermost desire that you familiarize yourself with both Marcus and Christopher, who are the two main characters in APIS, so that you fully enjoy the book that you are about to read.

Should you desire to do so, you can order a copy, or copies, of **ANOTHER PLACE IN SPACE** directly @ **www.AnotherPlaceInSpace.com**. You can also check with some online booksellers and distributors, such as **www.BuyBooksOnTheWeb.com** or by going to **www.amazon.com** or from **www.bn.com**.

APIS was molded together in profound, yet delicate layers. It was created in FOUR PARTS. This leads the reader through a complete three-hundred-sixty degree metaphysical voyage. It was deliberately put together using a minimal amount of words so that one could ponder over the contents again and again... each time unfolding another stratum of the infinite possibilities that have yet to be discovered. It comes complete with full-page sketched illustrations and is in an easy-to-read font so that you can absorb the insightful concepts as you participate in the Spiritual Journey by using your imagination...

ANOTHER PLACE IN SPACE

PART ONE
A PLACE... IN SPACE...
[Inner Space]

A very High Realm that is located outside the dimensions of Outer Space... beyond the boundaries of your conscious mind. For lack of better words, "A PLACE... IN SPACE..." is to be found in what you could call INNER SPACE; far, far away and yet closer than the air that you breathe.

"A PLACE...IN SPACE..." is a beautiful utopia where the IMMORTALS reside.

The air is filled with a brilliant sound of music that can be seen and felt, as well as heard. Everything here is so fresh, so alive and so pure. The Immortals are so beautiful! They are sovereign, evincing and magnificent, giving out an aura that is brighter than you ever thought possible and yet not in the least way blinding. You see them so clearly. You are so close and yet you are distant, in the sense that you do not feel totally at one with them. They do not see you. They are unaware of anything that is less than perfect. And yet, they are aware, because deep-down, you are perfect. Their love overwhelms you! The words escape you! You are there! You are really there! Fascinating! Truly fascinating!

PART TWO
THE JOURNEY
[From Heaven to Earth]

Part Two takes you on a beautiful, systematic process of one Immortal descending from the aforementioned utopia and into the "Three Dimensional Earth Plane" which is better known as the Physical Dimension or Planet Earth.

This chapter guides the reader through the vibratory levels from one realm into the other as an individual Immortal or Soul, in Spiritual or Heavenly form, develops into an embryo and then a fetus as it transmutes into a physical shape and form while manifesting into the "Three Dimensional Earth Plane".

As the Immortal journeys into his conception on Earth, he appears to travel through a different level of vibration. Different sights, sounds, and sensations are very much a part of this experience. Now that he is semi-attuned to your "wave length", it is easier to put into words some of the extraordinary events that the Immortal is experiencing.

The visual effects are indeed stupendous! The sounds! The music! It is all so unquestionably aesthetic.

PART THREE
ANOTHER PLACE IN SPACE
[Earth]

An Immortal is born! This chapter fast-forwards to an elderly man by the name of Marcus who is in his eighties. He is lonely and is living alone since the death of his wife. As fate or chance would have it, so it seems, Marcus spots an advertisement in the Food Section of the newspaper.

This unusual ad is a cleverly devised poem in which another elderly man, by the name of Christopher, is seeking a place to stay for room and board. After some consideration of the matter, Marcus decides to telephone Christopher and the two of them meet to get acquainted.

Marcus and Christopher develop a great friendship as Marcus, a former Minister, learns many Spiritual Teachings from his friend. Marcus is also able to relive many memories with Christopher and share his poetry with him. The two men share hours and hours and days upon days of in-depth, philosophical discussions. They have many walks through the park; great dinners and weekly nights out at the local pub.

As death is a part of life, Part Three inevitably ends with the two friends perishing in a home fire. The cause of the fire is unknown.

PART FOUR
THE RETURN! THE REUNION! THE HEREAFTER!

The final chapter has several twists and layers to it that spark the imagination. Both, Marcus and Christopher ascend from the "Three Dimensional Earth Plane".

Christopher guides his dear friend as he announces that Marcus will soon be reuniting with his beloved wife, Mary Anne, who had crossed over into the Spirit World years ago.

Christopher foretells that Marcus will be resuming his career in a somewhat different capacity as he did, in former years, on Earth when he was a Minister.

8

Christopher instructs Marcus as the two men stand in what appears to be a valley, which is located in the Astral Plane or Higher Realm. For those of you unfamiliar; the Astral Plane is simply the next less dense plane to the Physical Plane of which Earth is a part of. The instructions given by Christopher are that Marcus will soon become a "Dharmacist"*. Similar to that of a Pharmacist who dispenses pills to get a body in sync when the person is sick; a Dharmacist dispenses true wisdom, or ideas, to get a Soul in sync when need be.

Marcus is elated with all that is being told to him by Christopher. After a while, to Marcus' utter amazement, he witnesses Christopher begin to vibrate, faster and faster as Christopher attunes to a higher frequency before disappearing in the midst of Marcus' eyes.

The incredible three-hundred-sixty degree meta-morphosis, or transformation, nears its end as Christopher transmutes beyond physical form, or appearance, and ventures to a Higher Realm which is beyond the Astral Plane. Christopher travels all the way back outside of time and space. He goes back to where the beginning of this story began. Truly, a Metaphysical Adventure!

THE SOURCE, the book that you are holding in your hand, continues where "APIS" left off. At first, you will be guided into the dimension where Marcus and his wife, Mary Anne, reside. You will then experience their "lives" and those that they interact and live with.

Enjoy the journey.
Love, Light and Insight

Edward

January 13, 2005

Edward Namerdy coined both "Dharmacist" and the definition of the word in February of 1984.

The definition of a Dharmacist: "A living soul, in flesh or beyond, who dispenses wisdom or high ideals and teachings to help others to become Spiritually attuned to One's greater purpose and ultimate destiny."

The character, Marcus, a Dharmacist, was first mentioned in the novella, **ANOTHER PLACE IN SPACE**.

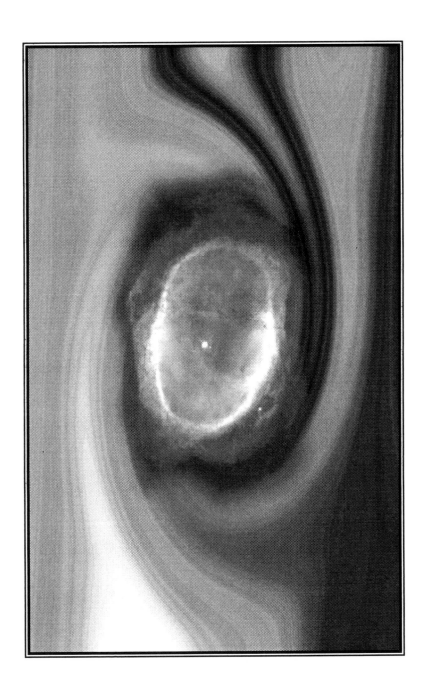

You are embarking on a fantastic journey beyond the "Three Dimensional Earth Plane". You quickly swirl through the portal which tunnels from one dimension to another. There is a familiar, heavenly, smell of perfume or incense.

As you travel, you are subdued by the experience, yet in awe of the beautiful lights that are gently racing by.

In the distance you see a bright glowing object... a sphere of some kind. It is spectacular to view. The colors are multi-dimensional. You can reach out and seem to be able to touch the atmosphere as you appear to merge with it. It is, literally, indescribable in worldly terms of that on Earth.

You hear sounds that are spellbinding, and, yet, you feel safe and secure... totally at peace.

There are harmonic overtones which seem to penetrate to the very core of your inner being. This gives you a feeling of renewed assurance that you are in atonement with this beautiful and most tranquil experience.

As you reach this other world, this "New Dimension", you feel rejuvenated. You are able to scan a wide area of this land. The air consists of translucent spirals that contain the most beautiful pastel colors. The indescribable clouds in the sky are spectacular to observe. The mountains are majestic while the incredible valleys are absolutely breathtaking. The rivers are pristine with rippling currents. It is surely a wondrous land.

Listen to the harmonic tones that emanate from within this Higher Realm. The sounds are similar to chanting, simultaneously intertwined with the distant sound of soothing music, which is in rhythm with the atmosphere. There is such serenity present throughout this land. You are in a state of tranquility... remaining totally transfixed.

You are bearing witness to the Higher Realms. These Realms are every bit as real as the "Three Dimensional Earth Plane". They emanate from "*THE SOURCE*", as does all consciousness. These Realms vibrate at a higher frequency than the Physical Dimension, yet they are interconnected, and one necessitates the other.

At times, words will be used in figurative terms rather than literal terms. Keep in mind that the Higher Realms that you are experiencing are not in Outer Space. Everything in Outer Space is an outer manifestation of Inner Space.

The Higher Realms, or Interior World, exists in the "Universal Mind". These Realms can be accessed, or tapped into, through the deep recesses of the mortal mind. This process is made possible since there is an ongoing connection between the Universal Mind and the mortal mind.

Prophets and Seers, throughout the ages, have tapped into the Universal Mind or the Interior World.

The Universal Mind is always speaking to the mortal mind. It is the mortal mind which has taken a blind eye and a closed ear to the Universal Mind; due to the distractions of the exterior world. This is why meditation or reflection is of the utmost importance.

The Higher Realms are, most often, far beyond your conscious awareness and focus as there is only so much that the conscious mind can comprehend.

With patience, understanding and practice; the mortal mind can learn to quiet itself and converse with the Universal Mind.

The Higher Realms are reality in its purist and finest form of manifestation.

Reflect on these things for a while. Merge with this Land and become a part of it. Remember, for you have been here before.

IMAGINE! JUST IMAGINE!

You continue to observe that the air consists of translucent spirals that contain the most beautiful pastel colors.

Numerous spiral patterns are also reflected in the overall architecture of the city which is now coming into view. Many of the buildings are dome shaped with a superimposed spiral pattern. Some structures are of a pastel looking marble. You sense, from deep down within your very soul, that these, seemingly, sacred and magnificent buildings are very essential.

These marvelous buildings are filled with the knowledge of the ages to help the inhabitants in the development and evolution of their souls. Relax as you become immersed in the Love and Harmony that surrounds you.

You realize that these souls, who, having departed the "Three Dimensional Earth Plane", now inhabit these Higher Realms, and have lessons to learn the same as they did while on Earth.

This Realm, as Heavenly as it may be, is not the final resting place for all. There is still work to be done here, as there is on Earth.

The entities here, from now on referred to as "Immortals", are at different levels of consciousness.

The one common bond that these Immortals have is that they are on the same wavelength with regard to the vibration that they are attuned to. This is similar to being on the same radio frequency. The Immortals are all of good intent and spirit in this Higher Realm.

The Astral Plane, which consists of Higher Realms and Lower Realms, is every bit as vast as the Physical Plane, the place you know as Earth ["Another Place In Space"]. Entities in this "Plane" of existence are where they belong, based on their conscious level and belief system. There are Heavens, and there are Hells, within the Astral Realms.

You will focus on the Higher Realms of the Astral Plane. You would not want to visit the Lower Planes of the Astral Plane any more than you would want to visit the Lower Places on Earth.

Be at peace and relax as you dwell in the Higher Realms... the Lighter Realms... Take solace in the fact that you, along with the Immortals, are here for a very important and meaningful reason.

Now, it is time for a visual exercise before observing some of the Immortals.

Take a deep breath through your nose and hold it for a few seconds. Now release it slowly, out of your mouth, as you soak in the beauty and transformation of your total being.

Open up the doors of your mind while you imagine a

source of pure White Light surrounding you. This White Light is protecting you. This Light can be seen and felt if you are creative. Be creative.

The Light begins from within you. At first it is about one inch in diameter as it begins to grow bigger and bigger in circumference until, finally, it envelopes you while it eventually radiates through your entire body encompassing your total being.

This Light becomes a Life Force or "élan vital". The Light is brighter than the Earth's Sun and yet the rays are not of the physical dimension. Its rays cannot burn you. The Light cannot blind you. The rays cleanse you! The rays encompass you!

These everlasting rays are radiating a sense of tranquility. The illustrious shafts of light are unequivocally outstanding. These glorious beams of energy that emanate from *THE SOURCE* are awe inspiring.

You and the Light blend as ONE. You and *THE SOURCE* are ONE. Let loose as you bask in the Light.

IMAGINE! JUST IMAGINE!

Now, the time has come for you to familiarize yourself with some of the Immortals and this wondrous Place. In Earth time, it has been over twenty years since the transition from planet Earth to the Astral Plane. Marcus, a retired Minister while on Earth, is totally focused on his new career and his sense of purpose. It was foretold to Marcus, by Christopher, that he would resume a career of helping souls to become enlightened. His good friend, and teacher, mentioned that he would become a "Dharmacist".

There are more Dharmacists in this Higher Realm of the Astral Plane then there are Pharmacists on Planet Earth. The two are very similar occupations. While a Pharmacist dispenses medicine to help get a person's body in sync, a Dharmacist conveys thoughts, ideas, and wisdom, to get an entity's soul in sync. So, you see, some of the Teachers in these Higher Realms that you will be focusing on, are also known as Dharmacists.

IMAGINE! JUST IMAGINE!

Marcus, a Dharmacist, is still teaching by preaching as he did while on Earth. He is still very much alive. He is still very much the same Marcus as he was back on Earth. He has reunited with his lovely wife Mary Anne. They had been together for thirty-four years while on Earth and are back together sharing their undying love for one another.

"We will meet again my dear friends," Marcus told his class, which is drawing to an end, in his soft- spoken voice. "We will meet again, soon."

Marcus' aura, as it is, in its present state, is most exhilarating. It starts at the base of his head... a deep-dark salmon that blends into a sunny yellow and ends with a geranium purple. It is quite a sight to see, the way it glistens as part of his energy field.

The class quietly disperses and goes on their way to their various classrooms that they are assigned to.

The beautiful marble structure, which serves as a school, seems to have an indescribable pastel spiral pattern that appears to glow from within the marble from which the building is constructed. Ostensibly, there is an inner source of energy that is coming from within this Heavenly structure.

"Well, I have done my work for today," Marcus thought to himself, while gathering his materials on his desk.

Marcus was in his eighties, in Earth terms, when he made his transition to the Higher Realm. One can plainly see that, in appearance, Marcus looks to be in his late forties. He no longer wears eyeglasses and his hair is a golden brown. While on Earth, through the years, his hair had gone from brown to a mixture of brown and white.

"Good day to you, Shirley. How are you? And, how is Clark?" Marcus asked, while walking home after his day at school.

"Clark is doing quite well... me too... He has been working with his new designs," Shirley responded, "He has manifested several hundred glorious new outfits. He is really getting good at it."

"Glad to hear it. And, tell Clark that I will be coming around to see him, soon. Are you still making gardens?"

Marcus wanted to know.

"Funny you should ask. I will be over with some ideas for Mary Anne as soon as I get the chance," Shirley replied as her radiant smile sent goodness to Marcus' Soul.

For you see, in this Land, so-called material things, such as; buildings, clothing and gardens are made from ideas, thoughts or inner beliefs. The beautiful buildings in the Higher Realms emanate from THE SOURCE yet they come into existence and are made real by the thoughts of the inhabitants and the inhabitants before them.

Everything in the Higher Realms first began with the consciousness of collective Souls that are either here now, or were focused here at some other time.

"All right, then, Shirley. I will pass your intentions on to Mary Anne, and I thank you. See you soon."

"Bring Clark with you if he can make it by. We always love you both and your company. It has been a while since we all got together," Marcus said.

"We shall do so, my friend." Shirley repeated, "We shall do so."

"I look forward to it, Marcus. But, wait! Let me 'Think' you some flowers to take home while we are together."

"I would love that," he replied.

Shirley is one of the most focused Immortals this Realm has ever witnessed, with regard to manifesting anything to do with gardens. Her presence of mind, along with her will, is so acutely attuned that she can create a bouquet of flowers in a matter of moments.

Her talent is second to her beauty. Shirley has a stunning complexion and long, flowing hair. Her aura reveals a soothing, light purple with a white outer band along the edge of her profile.

Shirley became silent. She went into a still-state of consciousness. Going into what you would call a still-state, or a meditative state, was easy for her to do being as well-trained as she was. Marcus watched this incredible manifestation of a beautiful floral bouquet.

"Voila! Take these," she said, while presenting the flowers to Marcus.

"You are amazing, Shirley," Marcus said with a smile. "They smell great too!"

"Yes, they do," she replied.

"You are more than kind, my dear, and I thank you on behalf of Mary Anne and myself. She will love them." Marcus took the flowers as they both departed on their various ways.

Marcus loved his walks from the school to his home. It gave him a chance to reflect on matters of concern, as he did lots of his thinking while he walked.

Once again you observe that the landscaping, consisting of flowers, trees, shrubbery, along with the sidewalks and streets, all emit this spectacular inner glow about them. Coupled with this is the beautiful Auric Field that encompasses and seems to permeate everything.

"**H**ello, my dear. I am glad you are home," remarked Mary Anne, as she greeted Marcus when he approached the entrance to their abode.

Both, Mary Anne and Marcus mentally projected rays of pink light around one another as a token of their devotion and love that they shared.

This wonderful light could be seen as it permeated them with sensations of warmth and goodness.

Mary Anne looked as though she was in her early thirties, which was the appearance she most remembered of herself while in the "Three Dimensional Earth Plane". She was small-framed with a wonderful smile, glimmering blue eyes and golden brown hair.

Their house is of a satisfactory proportion, dome shaped with the spiral patterns that emanate from all the buildings throughout this Higher Realm. It is ultraviolet in color with a smooth, graded appearance similar to that of the cobblestone walkway that leads to the front door.

"I am too. I am too," he repeated, as he walked up and gave his wife a warm embrace and gentle kiss.

Mary Anne noticed the bouquet of flowers.

"Oh, those are beautiful, Marcus."

"They are from Shirley. She said to tell you that she will be by soon." He handed the flowers to his radiant looking wife.

"Mary Anne, have you been in communication with anyone on Earth today?" asked Marcus.

Note, that the word "today" is figurative. You will remember that *"At times, words will be used in figurative terms rather than literal terms".*

The Immortals continue to speak, although their reality, with regard to Time, Space and Material Substance is quite different.

There are advantages and disadvantages that come with the frequency differences between the "Three Dimensional Earth Plane" and the Higher Realms. This will become clearer to you, the observer, as your observations unfold.

"Yes dear. I have, Marcus. I was in contact with

Sawyer again. He has become much more receptive in his communication with our Realm. He has become quite keen."

Mary Anne walked into the house with Marcus and together they took a seat.

Sawyer is a thirty year old taxi driver who lives in the Southeastern part of the United States. He has been attending Spiritual Studies Classes and is becoming very proficient in communication with the Higher Realms due to his desire, perceptivity and motivation.

"Sawyer is getting better at keeping notes and writing down the thoughts and impressions that come to him," Mary Anne commented.

Take notice that Mary Anne has a most dynamic aura about her, unlike any other you have seen. It seems to go from pastel pink, to a light yellow, to a lime green, to powder blue, and back to pink. She radiates Goodness and sparkles with positive energy.

"When Sawyer raises his level of vibration closer to ours, I am able to feel his thoughts so clearly. The trouble is that dear Sawyer has a difficult time realizing that the communication is from me. He often gets confused and thinks that it is his thoughts that he is hearing, because he hears them in the sound of his own voice. So, he tends to misinterpret his thoughts with the thoughts that are coming from me," she went on.

"He is getting much better at it, though," Mary Anne declared. "I envision that, in a few more years, Sawyer will be a tremendous help to many Souls who dwell on Earth."

Mary Anne, who crossed over to this Higher Realm several years before her husband, has become quite adept in communicating with people living on Earth. She is a Medium to Medium, of sort, for many Souls that have transmuted and are now conscious in the Higher Realm.

There are Mediums in this Higher Realm, as there are Mediums on Earth. On either side, these Mediums are a go-between, or a conduit for other Souls that wish to contact loved ones in other Realms. Many entities lack the sensitivity or know-how to do so. Some of these Mediums, within the Higher Realm, can raise their awareness, thus, being able to communicate with the many Higher Realms, as well as the "Three Dimensional Earth Plane".

These Mediums can transmit and receive messages through the finer, or ethereal, waves of existence as well as the denser waves such as on the Earth Plane. It is all a matter of reception and perceptivity. For you see, anything and everything in the far reaching Universe and beyond, begins in the Universal Mind, and is then passed down into individual consciousness.

"Sometimes, when Sawyer is sleeping, we carry on some great conversations. Unfortunately, he doesn't remember them when he awakens," Mary Anne, laughed out loud and added, "at least not consciously, anyway."

"Are you ready to partake in some food, Marcus?"

Marcus sat there, mesmerized. His eyebrows were raised an inch above their normal position, after having listened to his lovely wife explain the trials and tribulations of being a Medium.

"That would be nice, Mary Anne. Let us give Praise and enjoy some refreshment."

Food and drink in the Higher Realms is similar to that in the "Three Dimensional Earth Plane". However, the composition of refreshment is that of a different nature. What seems to resemble fluffy grains, luscious berries and tasty liquids are all part of the experience.

The primary difference is that the Souls do not partake in celestial foods out of necessity.

These celestial foods are a way of making some of the Immortals feel at home, like in their mortal lives in the "Three Dimensional Earth Plane". Again, it is not so much a necessity as it is the satisfying of an urge from a fading memory of the past.

Of course, in the Higher Realms, there are no grocery stores and there are no vegetable gardens, per se. On occasion Immortals may come across a blueberry patch, fruit bush or tree. However, most of the simple foods, such as has been described, are manifested within the ether waves through the thoughts of individual, or collective, consciousness.

There are even wines for those that have the desire to dabble. However, overindulgence is not compatible with the state of being of the inhabitants that dwell in the Higher Realms.

There is nothing to digest after partaking in food and drink, as the Higher Realm operates from a much finer and faster frequency level than that of the "Three Dimensional Earth Plane".

The Immortals eat very light, in both the literal and figurative sense. Some abstain from partaking in any bounty at all.

The misapprehension of food being a necessity passes quickly with most Immortals. Most of the Immortals learn that deep breathing techniques, chanting, and meditating are more nourishing than the ritual of partaking in celestial foods.

A class is just beginning in a rather large dome-shaped building, which rests gently upon a rolling hill. The handsome structure is located just beyond the lilac colored pond.

Ainsley, who is a scientist of sort, is conducting this class in "Unified Micro Affiliation".

Marcus is in attendance of this class as a student. It is not unusual for Dharmacists to attend one another's classes.

"It is of the utmost importance that we become attuned to the significance of our thoughts and aspirations," Ainsley tells her class in a soft-spoken voice.

"The celestial composition of our Souls is our gateway to '*THE SOURCE*'."

Ainsley appears to be in her twenties, although she has never lived within the "Three Dimensional Realm". Her Soul has been in existence for an Eternity without the desire to incarnate, or descend, into the denser Realms. Although Earth can be an excellent School and "Working Ground" it is not a place that every soul chooses to enter.

"May I ask you," Marcus wanted to know, "...is '*THE SOURCE*', that you made mention of, the same as 'Our Father, who art in Heaven'?"

"Yes, Marcus, they are one and the same. There are many titles and labels for the same thing." She continued, "Whether you call it the 'Grander Self', the 'Higher Self', the 'Truer Self', 'Christ Consciousness', or even 'Universal Consciousness', it is '*THE SOURCE*'."

"It is '*THE SOURCE*'," she repeated.

"We are gathered here to become 'Unified'. We are gathered here to synchronize," she avowed.

Ainsley continued with her teachings. She has a way of saying a lot with few words.

"I am not sure how many of you may have taken any kinds of Science classes while on Earth, but here are some scientific calculations. The Human body is composed of one hundred trillion cells, give or take a few billion. The physical body actually manufactures about a billion cells an hour." She paused for a moment as she eyed each Immortal in the room. "That is over sixteen million a minute or almost three hundred thousand per second."

"That boggles the mind!" Ethan yelled from the back row of the class. Ethan was another new resident to the Higher Realm, after having suffered a long-term illness before departing from Earth. His aura is far from clean or strong. Its color is a murky rusting brown which fades into a deep, reddish blue. This odd mixture of color is an indication that Ethan is still disoriented from his ordeal, but is recovering nicely.

"Yes indeed, Ethan, everything is in a state of constant change. It is never-ending," Ainsley confirmed to her students.

"It is my will to enlighten you all to the fact that right down to the last human cell of one individual Soul, we are all connected. Each and every cell in the 'Three Dimensional Earth Plane' stems from '*THE SOURCE*' and is in an ever-changing state."

She went on, "Getting back to a few more details, while on the subject, the human body manufactures a new stomach lining in less than a week... new skin in a month's time... an entirely new liver takes about six weeks... a new skeleton is completely formed within a matter of less than one hundred days... all new red blood cells in one hundred twenty days... Each person on Earth draws in new atoms with each and every breath that they take. They also absorb atoms through their skin. They breathe approximately twenty-thousand times in a twenty-four hour period..." Ainsley paused as she looked around the room at the different expressions on the faces of her students in the classroom.

"In the 'Three Dimensional Earth Plane' as well as our Higher Realm, Life is both Ever-changing and Everlasting. *'THE SOURCE'*, which is behind each and every cell in the physical anatomy, is also the source from which we stem." Ainsley paused briefly before asking the class, "Are there any questions before I draw this meeting to a close?"

"I have one, Ainsley. Well, actually it is more of a summarized evaluation of the information that you have transmitted to us," replied Joel, whose appearance is rather large in stature with a yellowish to orange, orange to reddish aura with a tint of steel blue finishing the outer regions of his energy field.

"Go right ahead with your question." urged Ainsley.

"You began today by reinforcing one's need to think harmonious thoughts. I gather that you are suggesting, by thinking the right thoughts, we, thereby, become closer to, or, are more aligned with *'THE SOURCE'*. And, that in doing so, this effects every Celestial cell in our body as thoughts also effect every cell in an Immortal's Human body, while they utilize the 'Three Dimensional Earth Plane'. Am I correct?"

"You are indeed, Joel. It all has to do with harmony. From the smallest cell in a human body, or, in the smallest Celestial cell in our 'Heavenly Bodies', there is a Divine connection to *'THE SOURCE'*. By thinking harmonious and pleasant thoughts, and with the right applications to our consciousness, we become more enlightened and synchronized in countless harmonious ways."

"Now, if that is all of the questions, I want to thank you for allowing me the opportunity of sharing these thoughts with you and I look forward to more discussions in the future." After a few moments of silence, the class began to disperse. Ainsley transmitted thoughts of peace and love to all of her students as they departed the classroom.

Ethan made his way down the curved hallway to his next class. He entered the large classroom and took his seat.

The entire building was filled with Dharmacists, or other sorts of Teachers, and Colorado was no exception.

Colorado is a thin-figured man, in appearance, who has taken on the name of the state where he used to reside while on Earth. He is good with analogies and an expert when it comes to the animals that dwell in the Higher Realms.

"I see a few of you are new to this class. When I call your names, please announce yourselves to me. Thank you." Colorado read from his list of new students.

"Charlotte!"

"Present."

"Geraldo!"

"Present, Sir."

"Patsy!"

"Present."

Colorado went on.

"Helena." He quickly corrected himself. "Helen, I mean."

"Here, I am."

"Sorry about that. I know a 'Helena'." The teacher continued.

"John."

"Here." Two voices responded in unison.

"Oh, there are two of you, I see. This is not the first time this has happened," Colorado recalled.

"Sir, my middle name is 'Patrick', so why not call me 'JP'? I often use my initials," one of the two men offered.

"'JP' it will be, then."

"Suzanne."

"Yes, over here."

Suzanne, a 'female vibration' formerly from France, was amazed at how she thought and spoke in French and yet it came out in English so the others could understand.

She was new to the Realm and was still adjusting to the fact that all languages are mere expressions of thought which come from *THE SOURCE.*

"All right class, I would like to discuss the nature of Pets in the Higher Realms," Colorado stated.

"...for today, cats, to be more specific..."

"I realize that some of you are new to this Realm and still are not familiar with – for those of you that have 'Pets' – why it is that your beloved critters keep vanishing."

You can hear the laughter in the classroom. Colorado has a good sense of humor. His feeling is that laughter is good for the Soul. Therefore, the Teacher was keen on making sure that his Students have a good time as they learn.

"Beloved former pets, from the 'Three Dimensional Earth Plane', such as a cherished cat, are present in the Higher Realms. However, the number of them is much more limited for reasons which are very complex to describe," Colorado paused. At times he seemed to go into a trance as he described the nature of animals in the Higher Realms.

"On Earth, a cat will come and go, in consciousness, by taking catnaps... often," he said, smiling.

"When an Immortal, while in human form, is communicating with a cat, on Earth, the pet will obviously be in a waking state."

"Similarly, when an Immortal, in the Higher Realms, wants to communicate with a pet, through one's desire, the pet will manifest."

"Unlike in the Physical Dimension, when there is a lack of interest of communication, the pet, in the Higher Realm, will vanish, in shape and form, and slip into a collective consciousness with its counterparts in lieu of what otherwise, on Earth, would have been a "catnap." Colorado picked up a flower from his desk and held it to his nose.

He went on and said, "Pets are willing to go in and out of individual consciousness providing the Love is reciprocal."

"Not to change the subject but, be assured that there is a similarity that many of the Immortals experience, with regard to sleep. There are varying degrees of the sleep-state that an Immortal, in the Higher Realm, encounters."

"When a deep-sleep state occurs, some of the more

advanced Immortals seem to decompose, in shape and form, while entering into a different level of vibration."

By this time Colorado was shifting his attention into the sleeping patterns and the varying degrees, of which the Immortals, in the Higher Realms, encounter.

Colorado shared his thoughts with the class. "The advanced Immortal soul can become engrossed and totally submerged in a supernatural and, at times, a most stimulating and collective consciousness."

"This is almost indescribable in words," Colorado avowed, as he went on with his speech.

"The aforementioned is only with regard to 'deep-sleep', which is easily undone through one's will." Colorado paused at this time as the class of students processed the information being transmitted to them.

Patsy raised her hand to get the Dharmacist's attention.

"Yes, Patsy?"

"What about dogs?" Patsy asked as she pointed out the window. A beautiful Springer Spaniel was running through the multi-hued pastel field that surrounded the building.

"We can discuss the loyalty and perceptivity of dogs at a later time... there are indeed great similarities," Colorado replied.

The topic of cats, and their connections, or "communication" with the Immortals continued until Colorado felt confidant that his students understood what was being said.

Marcus was on his way home, shortcutting across the pasture, when he took notice of Mary Anne playing in the field with their favorite dog.

"Mary Anne? Mary Anne?"

The echo of Marcus could be heard across the beautiful meadow.

"I am here. Over here with Shelby." Mary Anne called out to her beloved husband.

The setting is absolutely divine. There is plenty of room for running and having fun.

For the most part, the overall climate is very calm and relaxing, without precipitation, except for the light mist that is in the air.

"I have been looking all over for you Mary Anne," Marcus cried out. "Good to see you too, Shelby." Marcus laughed while Shelby jumped up and gently put his two front paws on Marcus' stomach.

Shelby is a Springer Spaniel and the adopted pet of many who reside here. His loved ones on Earth mourned him when he came to the Higher Realms leaving them behind. He was taken in by a close friend of his owners who had come to this land recently. Shelby quickly became friends with many other Immortals shortly thereafter. He is glistening with a pinkish rose aura that suits him perfectly.

"I had the strangest dream a while ago," Marcus mentioned to his wife.

When in the Higher Realms, Immortals tend to go in and out of "dream states" in a different manner than in the "Three Dimensional Earth Plane".

"Please, tell me about your dream, Marcus. I have always enjoyed hearing about your dreams. They are often experiences being shown to you by your 'Higher Self'," she informed him.

"And, sometimes dreams are shown to you by your 'Lower Self', too," she said, laughing.

She went on to assure Marcus, "Interpretations of your dreams vary as your 'Soul Development' continues to unfold."

"Well, the sky was awfully dark and I became very

frightened," Marcus began to explain.

"I was utterly petrified," Marcus continued.

"Then, I saw the fire. It was everywhere. We were engulfed in it."

"The fire that you and Christopher were in... the fire where you died...?"

"Yes. I closed my eyes and said to myself, 'wake up, I must wake up'. It is only a dream. At this point I realized that I was dreaming." Marcus went on, "The 'creatures' that I saw were evil looking. They looked like dark shadowed silhouettes."

"A few of them tried to grab me. I heard strange noises, too... groaning and moaning..." Marcus tried to explain.

Mary Anne threw a ball for Shelby to fetch as she said, "That does sound pretty scary. I have been to places like that too."

She urged him on. "This is all the more reason why you should remember to think strongly of a beautiful 'white light' surrounding you with Love."

"Your idle time should always include envisioning a white light around you, until it becomes second nature to you, and you no longer have to think of it." Mary Anne watched Marcus' eyes closely, making sure that he understood, completely, what she was saying.

By this time, Shelby was running back with the ball. They repeated the playful exercise several more times.

Mary Anne tried to convince her concerned husband. "I can assure you that these dreams will become less and less common for you. There is nothing to be afraid of, Marcus."

"I sure hope you are right, Mary Anne."

"It is quite common to be afraid of the unexplained. These 'evil spirits' are 'thought forms' which are mere reflections of the horror that bestowed you and Christopher in that devastating circumstance."

She went on. "These dreams are a way of expelling your fears. They are a necessary occurrence, Marcus."

By this time Marcus was smiling and feeling much more secure.

Keep in mind that there are many Realms in the

Astral Plane. You are focusing on but one Realm of an infinite number. Other Realms have different situations with other experiences.

Envision, if you will, that all Realms of existence can be compared with the bands on a shortwave radio. Within each bandwidth there lies a different frequency stream.

Imagine how many different activities there are within each frequency alone. This gives you a clearer picture to the great degree in which Realities can vary within a Realm and/or from Realm to Realm.

The three of them went back to playing in the meadow and being thankful for their time together in this glorious land.

AND TIME ROLLED ON

In addition to Dharmacists, there are Immortals, such as Clark and his wife Shirley, mentioned earlier, who have the extraordinary ability to be able to manifest things, such as clothing and flowers, merely, by "willing" the item into existence.

It is a respected profession in these Higher Realms and it has these two Immortals very much in demand.

Shirley and her husband Clark are impeccable with their tireless and gifted abilities.

Clark can manifest an entire outfit as quickly as an Immortal can speak the words to describe what it is that they desire. Sometimes, he can even create a garment faster than that. When he is really focused, he can see an Immortal coming into view and miraculously know what it is that the Immortal wants in the way of a new outfit before the words are even spoken. It is amazing to observe such an event take place.

Clark is round figured and short in stature. His merry disposition makes it a pleasure to be in his presence. He is lightly balding on the crown of his head and his aura consists of deep magenta, flowing just above the frame of his shoulders and head, before fading into a lovely bluish medium gray.

"I know what you want. I can feel it in my bones," Clark said, smiling ear to ear, as Marcus approached him.

"How are you, Clark? It is always a joy to see you... You are looking well."

"I am glad to see you too, Marcus. Shirley made mention that you would be coming by."

Before Marcus can get the words out, Clark is manifesting a beautiful embroidered cloak for him. It is emerald green and soft to the touch.

"This will do fine for you... Here we go... In a little while I know you will want to change your 'look' again. Enjoy this nice cloak."

"I will send you over a few more items promptly. You like to change your outfits more than any Immortal I know," Clark chuckled.

"Thank you. It looks lovely," Marcus replied with a

smile. "This is true. I do like my cloaks."

Marcus is rapt with wonder as he gazes in awe at Clark's amazing ability to manifest apparel. His appreciation is clearly visible.

While living in the "Three Dimensional Earth Plane", Marcus, generally, wore somewhat drab colored clothing. Subsequent to his transformation to the Higher Realm, he has taken on a new persona with regard to his attire. It seems as though he is now drawn to crisp, bright colors with lots of embroidery.

"Come by with Shirley when you get a chance. We always love your company. We can 'Group Med'. It has been a while since we all got together," Marcus said.

"Group Med" is an expression, used in this Higher Realm, for the activity of "Group Meditation", when three or more Immortals engage in a formal procedure, or ritual, of meditating, collectively. Chanting and/or the declaration of an affirmation may take place during this process as well. When there are only one or two Immortals involved this is known as "Oneness-Alignment".

"We shall do that, my friend. We shall do," Clark repeated.

"Farewell, for now," Marcus replied as he went on his way, caressing his cloak with esteem.

AND TIME ROLLED ON

The Sphere glowed brightly in the sky, not blinding in the least way, unlike the Sun in the "Three Dimensional Earth Plane".

There are some Immortals who pray to the Sphere. They seem to worship it. Others, simply, "go within" themselves, when it comes to meditation or prayer.

It is common knowledge, in this "Land of the Immortals", that the Sphere has powers and is indeed something mighty.

Mary Anne is one who routinely uses the Sphere as a focal point with her work in Mediumship. To help herself come in contact with a Higher Realm or an Alternate Realm, she gazes upon the Sphere to become centered. After going into a meditative state; her clairvoyant, her clairaudient, and her clairsentient abilities engage. This glowing Sphere is quite unfathomable... and very mystifying.

Mary Anne's ongoing telepathic communication with her friend, Sawyer, is getting better all the time. Sawyer is becoming much more receptive. It has already been three years, in Earth time, since the two of them began their communication with one another.

Sawyer has now progressed to the point that he is now quite popular in his Realm with his Mediumship abilities and he no longer drives a taxi.

At present, Sawyer is conducting "Private Readings" for people and teaching "Spiritual Reunion" classes.

He has been communicating with the dead, so to speak. However, they were still very much alive, with the exception of having shed their physical bodies and moved past the "Three Dimensional Earth Plane".

Over in Everest Hall, a group of people have gathered in hopes of getting their "Hello" messages to their loved ones who were in the "Three Dimensional Earth Plane". Mary Anne works her Mediumship on her end while Sawyer cooperates at his end, on Earth.

"Attention Class. Can I please have your attention?" Mary Anne called out.

"I realize that some of you have traveled distant wavelengths, in thought, to be present here at this time."

Several of the Immortals that are attending Mary Anne's class, in "Mediumship Communication", are from other Realms. The travel from one Realm to another is simply a matter of focusing one's thought. What would have been a great distance to travel in the "Three Dimensional Earth Plane" is simply a brief, visual meditation... a focus on where it is that one wants to travel... This requires the will, desire and know-how to put this plan into action and it gets easier with practice.

"For those of you present, that have not attended one of my sessions, I am pleased that you are here. My name is Mary Anne and I am a 'Medium'."

She went on and explained, "I will be in communication with my counterpart, whose name is Sawyer."

The Immortals are seated in what resembles a theatre. In front of them is a gigantic oval shaped screen. It is a silvery, metallic looking object that seems to oscillate and is capable of displaying images from the "Three Dimensional Earth Plane".

It looks very much like a gateway or a portal with the exception of the fact that you can not walk into it. Nor, can you walk through it.

"Sawyer, who is now becoming visible on the screen, will be initiating any contact between the two Realms," Mary Anne continues to enlighten those who have assembled in Everest Hall.

Part of Mary Anne's Mediumship abilities enables her to be able to generate what is taking place in Sawyer's class on to the huge screen, so that the Immortals in her class can, as a group, participate in the communication process.

Mary Anne glanced up through the skylight at the intricate Sphere that is visible from where she is situated.

"What I ask for you to do, at this time, is to project your messages, thoughts or impressions on to the screen. Whatever you want to convey to your loved ones, do so now!" Mary Anne instructed her class. Her radiant glow subdued their emotions.

Back on Earth, Sawyer's group is contentedly seated in the circle which has been formed. Sawyer is standing in the middle of the group, rotating his position, from time to time, in order to look at each person in the room.

"Welcome. My name is Sawyer. I will not be able to give 'Spirit Messages' to each and every one of you this evening. We will see how things unfold. Please know that whether or not I am able to make contact with your 'loved one', personally, that does not mean that they are not aware of your interest in contacting them. You can do this at any time, on your own. Although they have laid down their physical body, they are still very much alive. You may want to consider speaking to them in your own personal way, at a time which is most suitable to yourself. When I conduct my Spirit Communication with the 'other side' my level of energy or vibration is raised. It is similar to turning up the speed on a treadmill. So, forgive me if I tend to talk a bit fast. I will try my best to speak with my voice elevated a bit and as clearly as possible."

Sawyer, who had a short-lived career as a model in years past, stands about six-foot, one-inch tall. His fine brown hair is long and pulled back in a ponytail.

"Coming from over here," looking directly at the back row toward a couple to his left, Sawyer said, "I am seeing 'spinning', a whirlpool of 'spinning',"

"Well, I…"

"Wait! Not yet!" Sawyer stopped a man from speaking.

"I have with me the 'energy' of a young girl… who I believe may have crossed over by drowning… is this correct?"

The couple in the back, where Sawyer had been focusing, responded to the question.

"Well, our neighbor had a pool party several months ago…"

"That's the one." Sawyer suggested before the man could finish his statement.

Meanwhile, back in the Higher Realm, at Everest Hall, the small Immortal has been projecting her energy on to the huge screen, as suggested. She knew that her parents back on Earth were devastated by her untimely demise. It is amazing to observe how both of these dimensions are able to communicate, indirectly, and get their important messages across via third, or even, fourth

43

parties. It all seems to come together for all concerned.

"This beautiful girl has come here this evening to get the message through to her parents that she is all right. She wants to assure them of this." Sawyer transmitted the information as it was being dispensed to him.

"I want to move across the room and over here," Sawyer stated, as he moved towards two people sitting there. They were twins.

"I see a male vibration... 'Harold'. I am getting the name 'Harold' and next to him is someone with the name of 'Emmy'. No, it is 'Emma'."

Mystified, as to be expected, one of the twins, in the area where Sawyer had been looking, spoke up in response.

"Yes. I have a Great Uncle named 'Harold'."

"Passed on?" Sawyer asked.

"Yes. And 'Emma' is his wife," remarked one of the twins. She was kind of like our nanny when we were younger."

"Well, they have come to let you know that they love you. They want to remind you that they are not dead." Sawyer laughed out loud as he relayed the message that he was receiving.

"They seem to have a nice sense of humor too," Sawyer pointed out.

"They always did," the other twin commented, holding back a tear, as she smiled.

"Well, they still do," Sawyer said softly, with a smile.

Over the next hour, in the "Three Dimensional Plane", or Earth time, a continuous flow of communication and messages went back and fourth between the two Realms.

In one Realm, you have the gifted abilities of Sawyer, who is able to receive, to process and to transmit information. In the other Realm, you have Mary Anne's talents of being able to transform information that was projected on to the screen and transmit the various thoughts to her counterpart, Sawyer. It is an incredible affair to witness as well as partake in.

As the session neared its end the images that were on the screen began to lighten while losing their contour.

The Mediums, Mary Anne and Sawyer, drew their sessions, that had taken place in both Realms, to an eventual halt. At the close of the exciting meetings, both audiences simultaneously disbursed.

AND TIME ROLLED ON

A flock of pure white doves seems to float in celestial air, as they fly, slowly, over the lilac pond.

There, Marcus is lazily daydreaming, as he gazes at the rippling water, before going to conduct his class in "Coexisting Dimensions".

"True wisdom is becoming attuned to what you already know deep, deep down inside." The words of his old friend, Christopher, were coming to his mind.

"The more 'inner truths' unfold to me the more I agree with that profound statement," Marcus thought to himself. "Surviving my former existence on Earth was a divine unfoldment in and of itself,"

"I used to pray to the Lord while I looked outwardly for answers. Now, I can truly say that I 'Dwell in the House of the Lord' as I have shed my Physical Body and come to realize that what was 'inside' of my Physical Body was the 'inner me' and 'inner' is all that I have... we must keep going inward as we dwell in the house of the Lord," Marcus revealed to himself.

"Every thought that an Immortal has – be they on Earth or in the Higher Realm – produces a vibration or a ripple." Marcus' thoughts were shifting while he focused on the ripples in the pond.

"So, 'True Wisdom' is becoming attuned to what 'I' already know deep down inside," he said to himself as he made his way to his feet. "I had better be on my way."

Marcus drew in a deep breath and held it for a few moments allowing the ethereal waves to permeate his entire being.

After making his way to the campus, Marcus entered the classroom where his Immortal students were waiting for their course to commence.

Marcus addressed his learners, "It is glorious to be here. Let us begin, shall we."

"I am aware, from the previous conversations that we have had, that although all of you have lived on Earth at one time or the other... most of you are new to this particular 'Higher Realm'. Is this correct?"

After a few nodding of heads and "Yes Sir's", Marcus proceeded to speak.

"I would like to continue on with our discussion on the similarities between Immortals in our realm and that of the Immortals that dwell in the "Three Dimensional Earth Plane.""

"When I first made my transition to the Higher Realm, I was quite disoriented. For what seemed like a year or so – although, I do not know how long it was for sure – I had trouble realizing that I was still the same Soul that I had been while on Earth... Not that much had really changed in that regard... that is to say, 'not that much' in the way of personal identity." Marcus eyed the room full of students.

The auras of the students, that are present in the room, vary from that of crimson red, to gold, to orange, to blue and to green. There is also a predominant misty yellow that filled the ethereal waves. This is due to the interaction and exchange of information that is, at the same time, being processed by those who are in the room.

Marcus went on, "Eventually, I was enlightened to the self-realization that I was never actually a 'Human Being', although my Soul had taken on a human form. My physical body was an outer garment to my Soul just as my Soul is an outer garment to the Holy Spirit or the essence of eternal life.

The real inner-self -- which was utilizing the 'tool' known as the 'physical body' -- is what you see and hear now, standing in front of you, conversing.

I still take on a human-like form, yet, I am not a human. I am a Spiritual Being as I was while in the 'Three Dimensional Earth Plane'.

I occupied a physical body while..."

Marcus was interrupted by an untrained, yet humble, soul by the name of Jason.

"You were never 'human'?" Jason asked with concern.

Jason is a new soul, one who has an undeveloped consciousness, in the sense that he lacks the recall of his prior incarnations. He still has no conception of what he is, or what he is doing here, in this Realm, or where he is going. Jason's previous incarnations were like repeating the same grade in school again and again, although his glimpses of a higher awareness are improving.

Furthermore, Jason lacks the perceptivity, sensitivity and the atonement of being able to dwell deep within the essence of his total being. He is in need of being able to develop the ability of being still, so as to listen to his inner-voice.

"Jason, if I may continue... We are all individual Souls with 'individual consciousness', who are Immortal. We were never 'Human Beings', per say. We were merely Souls, as we still are, who chose to have a mortal, or temporary experience, in another dimension. We took on, or should I say, we entered a physical body when we entered the 'Three Dimensional Earth Plane'. Whether in this Realm or in that Realm... We are merely, 'Souls' who are having experiences. Some of these experiences are important lessons to us while some of these experiences are not."

"I enjoyed the message that you shared in our last class, and I am still dwelling on its symbolism." An angelic voice could be heard from the center of the room.

Amethyst is a stunning looking creature whose violet aura goes well with her name. Visibly, one can notice that Amethyst vibrates at an extremely high frequency level due to her acute sensitivity.

"And what was that my dear?" Marcus asked.

"Well, I will quote what you said, 'Keep your thoughts in Spirituality... Keep your feet in Reality... Keep your heart in-between'," she said, while smiling to her classmates, "That is it, word for word."

She commented, "I have gone over that statement many times in my thoughts. I see great wisdom in those words. Although it was written with the human form in mind, it still rings true."

"Those words were given to me while I was on Earth and I was never able to trace the exact origin of who said them. I used to end my sermons with that phrase," Marcus responded.

"I have attempted to 'attune' to the 'Akashic Records' to see who it was, or where, the author of those words may be. My efforts, thus far, have been to no avail," Marcus continued.

"Yes, you can apply those great words of wisdom in Earthly terms as well as here, in the Higher Realms. The message is to always focus on the Divine, or the 'Higher Grounds', while still remaining focused on where you are at the same time, thereby creating a harmonious balance. This is 'The "Key to Attunement'," Marcus explained.

"We are here today to learn to 'attune' to *'THE SOURCE'*."

Another student inquired. "Marcus, what are the 'Akashic Records'?"

"The 'Akashic Records' hold all of the information, handed down throughout the ages, and is stored in the form of 'vibrations' within the ethereal waves." He reiterated to the entire class, "Anything and everything that has ever occurred is stored in the 'Akashic Records' for all Eternity."

Marcus continued. "You utilized the 'Akashic Records' when you scanned through your previous life while doing your 'life-review'." Marcus' students seemed to thoroughly enjoy his teachings or they would not be present in the classroom.

The Immortals are not required to participate in any classes. Freewill, or self-rule, is vital within the Higher Realms. The only prerequisite for attending a particular class is for, and by, one's motivation and desire.

"If I may go back to what I was saying about life as we know it and life as we knew it," Marcus resumed his talks with his class.

"Envision, if you will, the anatomy of your Soul. In its truest form it is pure light... pure intelligence... pure love... pure beauty."

"We are all facets of the same glowing light from which we all stem... from which is within us all... Most of us have had experiences which allowed us to take on an outer layer, or a cocoon of sort, which also is known as the mortal body, while incarnating into the 'Three Dimensional Earth Plane.' When we passed through the veil of so-called death, we shed our cocoon, or our physical body.

Basically, there was a mental process, upon our departure from the 'Three Dimensional Earth Plane', which brought us to where we are as I hereby convey this to you. As it has been said; 'Birds of a feather flock together'. This, in turn, brings us to where we are, precisely, which some mortals would call Heaven," Marcus went on speaking.

"The Alchemy of a Soul is indeed a marvelous revelation."

The entire class listened attentively as they processed what Marcus was saying to them.

"The more One spends in meditation and deep collective, conscious bliss... the more One departs from the illusion of separation from one another. We are all part of a greater reality. Marcus completed his train of thought, "We have been and will always be."

The class continued as questions were raised and answers were delivered.

"I feel like since I left Earth I went from 'Level One' to 'Level Two' in a Video Game – which by the way, I played a lot of Video Games down on Earth," a student, named James cried out from the back of the room.

"Not a bad analogy," Marcus replied.

"However, you did not get to your so-called 'Level Two' merely by leaving your body in so-called 'Death'. There was divine harmony in the proper vibratory transition to where you are at this time based on lessons that were learned while on Earth and pertinent applications and deeds. In simpler terms... you are where you are at this time for a reason," Marcus avowed.

And, yet another student by the name of Travis gave his profound evaluation on reality.

"When I meditate, I can focus myself so that I am coexisting in a hologram of a sort... I am still in the 'Three Dimensional Earth Plane' the way that I was when I had my mortal body. Yet, I am here with this class in my Astral body. And, when I meditate further I am yet in a Higher Realm then this one... all simultaneously... it is all happening in layers that are intertwined... as I mentioned; as if I were inside a hologram or something," Travis shared his thoughts.

"Travis! That was a very good example of 'Coexisting Dimensions'. You have given the class much to ponder. I thank you for sharing your thoughts," Marcus stated.

"Well, class, it has been enlightening to be here with you all. We have exchanged some wonderful thoughts. I want to remind you to keep up with your meditating, collectively with friends as well as individually. Our Creator is within us. Always remember this," Marcus looked with intensity, yet with passion, at his students.

"I would like to close our discussion with another one of my poems," Marcus gestured with his hands as he gazed at the center of the room.

> *"The Immortals are here…*
> *The Immortals are there…*
> *They seem to leave, with us,*
> *Impressions to share…*
> *Although, they are here for only a while…*
> *They are here for Eternity,*
> *Each, with their own style…*
> *So, let us learn to count the ways…*
> *Let us make use of our wisdom,*
> *Throughout all of our days…"*

After finishing the poem Marcus looked toward his class while taking a deep breath and releasing it into the ethereal waves with an AUM sounding chant.

Marcus envisioned a brilliant white light that surrounded his class and became visible to them. The room brightened up with this magnificent pure, white light. The illumination could also be felt as it penetrated into the soul of each of the students that bared witness to this glorious manifestation.

"Keep working with the light. Use pink light for sending out love… use white light for sending out goodwill and harmony… keep working with the light," Marcus intoned.

"Well, class, it is time, once again, to bid you a fond farewell for now." Marcus repeated the phrase that was used by many as a blessing of sort. "We will meet again my dear friends. We will meet again, soon."

The students said their goodbyes and went on their way. Several proceeded to other classes while others went on to other regions within the Realm.

It is the dawn of a glorious day with the sound of music in the air. The scent of gardenias blowing across the meadows creates a relaxing atmosphere in Mary Anne's and Marcus' abode. The multi-colored sky of orange and turquoise seems to oscillate, ever so subtly. The color tones change from color to color in spite of the absence of the light of the Sun or the darkness of the Moon. Truly, it is breathtaking to live in this wonderland.

Mary Anne is diligently reassembling one of the crimson veils that decorate the Gazebo located in the backyard. She loves to watch the various colors of these veils as they wave in the gentle breeze.

"There, now, that should do it," Mary Anne said to herself as she finished with what she was doing.

"Stay here!" she cried out to Shelby.

The Springer Spaniel was forever playing and had so much energy. He was about to run off into the meadow until he was ordered otherwise. He ran up to the step just beneath Mary Anne and sat down.

"Be a good boy, won't you?" she asked of him.

Shelby looked up at Mary Anne somewhat squint-eyed, as if to say "Please let me run. Pl-e-e-e-a-a-a-s-se..."

"Oh, you win, Shelby. Run. Go ahead and run as you so desire."

Shelby did not wait around for any more convincing. He happily took Mary Anne up on her offer and ran off into the wondrous meadow.

"It is time for 'the meeting of the minds'," Mary Anne could hear Marcus say as he walked toward her from their home.

"Oh, good, then they both are coming, Marcus?"

"Yes dear, finish up as they will be here shortly."

Clark, and his lovely wife, Shirley, were expected to arrive at any moment for their "Group Med".

"We can all gather here in the Gazebo. They both like it out here and the Sphere is so awe inspiring at this time."

"I agree!" Marcus exclaimed, "Out here it shall be then."

When Clark and Shirley arrived, the four good friends gathered out back, near the Gazebo.

To help Mary Anne beautify the surroundings, Shirley began waving her arms and hands over the flower garden.

"I become absolutely mesmerized whenever I observe your transmutations in action. It is simply magical," Mary Anne commented to Shirley.

Shirley was miraculously manifesting a number of new varieties of flowers and brightening up the colors, for a change of pace. The "Heavenly Scent" became that much more acute during this transition.

"I do have a knack for gardens," Shirley responded, amusingly, in-between her diminutive chants that she was implementing. "Listen to them singing. You can hear the flowers intone."

The harmonic sounds that emanated from the array of flowers were soft, yet they could indeed be heard.

While engaged in nonchalant conversation, Clark and Marcus walked over and seated themselves in the Gazebo. Clark had been extremely busy manifesting clothing for countless beings on an ongoing basis. It was nice to retreat and be at peace with good friends.

"Where is Shelby?" asked Clark.

"He is out in the meadow again. Perhaps he is running with the unicorns. Sometimes I think that Shelby imagines that he is a unicorn," Marcus responded with that trademark expression of his... his eyebrows rose one inch above their normal position.

"You may have a point there," Clark chuckled.

Shirley and Mary Anne made their way back to the Gazebo to rejoin their husbands while Mary Anne thanked Shirley for the metamorphoses that she had performed in the garden.

After a while all four friends were comfortably seated in a circle, in lotus type positions, on some soft cushions.

The meditative state that the four friends were about to enter is known as a state of *STILLNESS*.

This is simply a method of stilling the mind; relaxing and focusing on imagery that the mind wants to envision or create.

The positive affirmation is: "*I AM STILL.*"

Mary Anne was facing so that she could look up toward the Sphere when she so desired. Everyone's palms were turned upright to symbolize reaching toward the Higher Realms.

"What is going to be our focal point for our 'Group Med'?" asked Clark.

"Marcus and I had discussed the idea of focusing on the Sphere this time. Would that be acceptable with the two of you?"

"That is all right with me," Clark said, while stretching and sitting up straight.

"Yes, the Sphere is a good idea," Shirley answered with a beaming smile.

Mary Anne began the Meditation.

"Alright, now take a deep breath through your nose and hold it... now, gently release it, letting it out through your mouth..."

She went on... "*I AM STILL.* Once again we are joined to form a union and to blend as 'One'."

Their surroundings began to fade as the four took long deep breaths, ever so slowly, as they went deep within themselves.

"We feel the rhythm of the Almighty Sphere. We hear the rhythm of the Almighty Sphere. We attune to Almighty Sphere that is above us."

Deeper and deeper they went...

"We are 'One' with the Sphere. We are 'One' with each other... We are within the Sphere and the Sphere is within us."

The four friends had become used to meditating together. They were adept in merging their consciousnesses and seemingly becoming One with each other in their "Group Med" sessions.

Marcus was softly chanting "*A-u-m*" sounds as the others joined in periodically. Chanting was an effective tool in uplifting the vibratory rate of the Soul. It also aided in bringing the Group into Spiritual synchronization with one another.

"*A-u-m-m-m-m-m-m-m...   A-u-m-m-m-m-m-m-m...*" The Group chanted in unison.

"A-u-m-m-m-m-m-m-m-m... A-u-m-m-m-m-m-m-m..."

During all of the chanting Mary Anne opened her eyes, ever so slightly, to glance at the Mystical Sphere.

To her astonishment, she noticed that she appeared to have relocated and become 'One' with the Sphere. It was as if Mary Anne was bi-locating. Although, she was still seated next her friends by the Gazebo, instead of seeing the Sphere in the distance, she saw an aerial view of the Gazebo with the four of them sitting on the floor.

"Well, I'll be..." she uttered a bit taken aback.

Mary Anne closed her eyes for a moment before reopening them.

This time Mary Anne was back in her Astral Body, inside the Gazebo, looking up at the Sphere. The Sphere, now, had numerous Orbs, ultraviolet in color, that were rapidly swirling in close proximity to the illuminating Sphere.

With the measure of time, in this Realm, being unequal to that in the "Three Dimensional Earth Plane", it was difficult to approximate how much time had elapsed during the Group Meditation.

One thing was for sure. There was an instantaneous and recognizable, serene feeling of peace that penetrated to the core of each of the four friends during the meditation. This sense of well-being continued.

"Did we go up into the Sphere?" Marcus asked while regaining his faculties.

"I believe that we did," Clark replied.

"It is quite interesting, Clark. I did feel as though my body floated up to the Sphere. I saw beautiful blue lights spinning around. First they were swirling around me and then I was swirling around them," Marcus said.

Shirley was at a loss for words in her efforts to describe her amazing experience.

"What about you, Mary Anne? What happened with you?" her husband asked.

"I have a strong impression that all of us were drawn up into the Sphere. I could feel all of you up there with me." Mary Anne went on explaining, "I could also feel the presence of other entities with us. We were all communicating telepathically. It was as though we were enveloped in a force-field of Supreme Intelligence."

"I must say you are describing my experience," Marcus concurred.

"It was very exhilarating! It was so unusual and yet incredibly recognizable," Clark added.

All four friends were undoubtedly passionate about their cosmic journey into the Sphere. For as much as it was a new and enlightening experience, it also triggered distant memories from within each of them.

"I would like to add, that during our experience to the Sphere, I had a strong impression that we were in the presence of my old friend Christopher... my dear companion who perished with me in the fire on Earth... When we arrived here, Christopher told me of my future and how I would reunite with Mary Anne... informing me of how I would become a 'Dharmacist'... well, when Christopher vanished in front of my eyes... when I witnessed him ascend... I had the same eerie feeling surrounding me as I did when the four of us were in the Sphere... certainly you could feel the presence of something very omnipotent could you not? It was the first time I have had that feeling since I said goodbye to Christopher..." Marcus struggled to explain to his friends.

"As I stated, Marcus, I could also feel the presence of other entities with us," Mary Anne reiterated.

"Don't misunderstand me... I like getting together to meditate and visit with the two of you... To be honest with you, I found this meditation a bit disorienting. It's just; I don't really feel that I am ready for traveling to Higher Realms. I like it just fine where I am. I manifest clothes. That's what I do and I do it well," Clark said.

"Yes Clark. You are the best," Mary Anne assured her friend, "They all come to you for your garments."

"Do not worry, dear. We are not going anywhere. I, too, want to remain where we are for some time to come. I love manifesting gardens right where we are," Shirley consoled her disoriented husband.

"We will stick to relaxing meditations and remain right here next time," Marcus reassured the garment maker.

They all laughed, jovially, having resolved the direction of their future meditations together.

"We had best be on our way," Clark gestured.

As Shirley and Clark stood up, they bid their farewells to Mary Anne and Marcus and thanked them for the unusual time together.

"We shall meet again, my friends, we shall meet again," Marcus said with a pleasant smile.

After Shirley and Clark departed, Mary Anne and Marcus discussed what had become apparent in their meeting with their two friends.

"Shirley is a flower maker and Clark is a garment maker. I have concluded that they come to visit us out of the love that they have for us. I sense that we should keep our 'far away' traveling to ourselves," Mary Anne laughed with her husband.

"So be it," Marcus said as he gave his wife a hug while gazing up at the Sphere.

"I know where to find you Christopher. We will meet again my dear friend. We will meet again," Marcus thought to himself.

AND TIME ROLLED ON

Nora is an Embodiment Counselor at the Re-embodiment Center, which is located atop a bluff, overlooking a dazzling valley.

Nora is working with several Immortals who desire to reincarnate into the "Three Dimensional Earth Plane". This is quite a complex transformation that can take place in a multitude of different ways.

"So, it seems you are troubled and have difficulty sustaining in the Higher Realms?" Nora asked one of the patients whose name will go unmentioned.

The Immortal patient replied. "I keep drifting and spending most of my time in the Lower Realms, which I cannot seem to stay away from."

His aura is very crusty and short-cropped looking. He appears to be very disoriented and restless.

"There are still lessons on Earth for me. I am not ready for the Higher Realms. I want to go back. I have waited long enough," the Immortal explained.

"We have been monitoring you as you drift away from the Higher Realm. We see you fade in and out as you struggle to retain your senses. Another incarnation may be the thing that you need."

"I feel it is. There is so much I want to do. I really want to return to the Earth Plane. It is simply a shift of focus and an adjustment in the perception of time. We are multi-dimensional are we not?" asked the troubled Soul.

"Yes," Nora concurred.

"Yes, it is simply a shift of focus." She continued, "As you know, 'time' is very different in our Realm. Our measure of a day can seem a lot longer on some days than on others. A long-lived, resourceful life in the 'Three Dimensional Earth Plane' only seems like a long time while you are experiencing it. You will be back before you know it.

In the event that you choose to incarnate, we will send forth loving energy to surround you," Nora assured the weary Soul. "We will help guide your inner-self as best we can... as much as is allowed."

In this particular ward of the Re-embodiment Center, there are several Immortals that have been waiting a long time to return to Earth. They have gone through numerous 'Life-Review' progressions and self-evaluations.

Most of these Immortals are spending long periods of time lapsing from one realm to the next as they have difficulty staying focused.

These Souls are seated in a lotus position. You can see them practically fade away as they drift deeper in thought. It is if they are caught between frequencies. They are out of sync in a manner of speaking. They are either troubled souls that are "Earthbound", and have trials and tribulations to experience in the "Three Dimensional Earth Plane", or else they simply enjoy the denser realms and have lessons to encounter.

Seeing how these Immortals, of concern, have a strong will and desire to return to the Earth Plane, and have waited and planed for quite some time, it seems likely most of them will finally get to reincarnate.

There are other Immortals who are underdeveloped Souls that seem to become Earthbound after crossing over into the Spirit World. They are not able to sustain the Higher Realms for long periods of time. Often, they drift back to the "Three Dimensional Earth Plane" the way a piece of driftwood is often drawn back to the shore.

Very little planning goes into these Immortals' return to the "Three Dimensional Earth Plane".

Still, there are other Immortals in the Lower Realms that do not have the luxury of returning to Earth in order to learn other lessons and or be of service in that dimension.

You shall refrain from focusing on these other realms of existence. You will refrain further by ceasing, at this point, to focus on the Immortals that wish to reincarnate.

Know that the Immortals that are observed here are souls that have the freewill to decide whether to return to the "Three Dimensional Earth Plane" or not to return.

There are some Immortals that reincarnate to attain more knowledge, which in turn leads to evolving on a Spiritual level. The "Three Dimensional Earth Plane" is an excellent school for Spiritual growth.

There are also Immortals that actually regress or take a step backwards, so to speak, when they choose to reincarnate. To them it is akin to going into a thick jungle with many obstacles to be encountered.   They go back to the "Three Dimensional Earth Plane" to help other Souls rather then reincarnating there to help themselves.

Reincarnating requires an extreme mental process that is difficult to comprehend in words. Great Master Teachers have elected to reincarnate in the name of helping their fellow man.

Think on these things and know that all things lead to good. Know that the reasons for reincarnation are countless.

The steadfast visions were getting increasingly stronger as time went on. Marcus had come to the conclusion that the thoughts and impression that were coming to his psyche during his meditations were subliminal messages from his friend Christopher who dwells in a Higher Realm of existence. Marcus was now set upon the notion that he would be reuniting with his long lost friend.

Marcus had yet to hear his friend Christopher, audibly, although his presence had indeed been sensed.

Something was indeed brewing, even though Marcus was unable to discern exactly what it was.

"I simply love it here, Marcus." Mary Anne marveled at the breathtaking fields of splendor that they were walking through.

"I do as well my dear. I do as well," Marcus conceded, "Look at Shelby run. You would think he was a racehorse. He never seems to run out of steam," Marcus chuckled with amusement.

"This looks like a wonderful place to sit for a spell, don't you think, Mary Anne?"

"How about over there by the brook," she said, while pointing just ahead and to the left.

"It is ever so soothing by the water. I can meditate easier with those beautiful sounds emanating from the brook," she added.

"Whatever you wish, my dear," Marcus responded as the two of them make their way over to the selected location.

"I would like to try something interesting during our meditation, Marcus," she said while taking a position near the water.

"What did you have in mind my dear?"

"As I have told you, my communication with Sawyer has continued to develop quite nicely. I would like to see if I can attune to Sawyer's wavelength while you attune to your friend Christopher's wavelength. In so doing, we may be able to link both realms to our realm... we may be..."

Marcus, interrupting what Mary Anne was relating to him, interjected, "I understand completely what you are

63

conveying and I like your idea tremendously." Marcus was enthusiastic as he continued elaborating.

"We can begin our *STILL STATE* together... blending as One, like we do so well, and then we can expand our directions while we remain 'At One' with each other," Marcus added with a smile.

"Yes, yes," she replied.

"Perhaps we can merge to the point to where Sawyer is not only aware of my presence but of yours as well. Conceivably, Christopher will be aware of all of us."

Mary Anne was excited about the potential merger of consciousness from within three different realms.

After a bit more conversing on the subject Mary Anne and Marcus, being comfortably arranged, went into a state of stillness as they commenced to meditate.

"*I AM STILL.* I am comfortably arranged as I attune to my friend Sawyer in the 'Three Dimensional Earth Plane'. Yet, I remain transfixed in this realm with Marcus..." Mary Anne whispered aloud as she proceeded to go deep into her *Still State* of being.

"*I AM STILL.* I set my focus on my good friend Christopher who dwells in the Highest of Realms." Marcus turned his focus deep in thought to the consciousness of his old companion.

"Although I am focused on a Higher Realm, I remain in this realm with Mary Anne..."

Now, about ten feet apart from one another, Mary Anne focused on the "Three Dimensional Earth Plane", with all of its density, while Marcus focused on a Higher Realm which is a lighter, less dense, realm then the one that he is in.

Like the frequency bands on a radio... Mary Anne's focus goes one way while Marcus' goes another...

Since the Higher Realms vibrate on a different frequency level then that of the Earth Plane; the concept of time operates under metaphysical laws that are unlike those of the "Three Dimensional Earth Plane".

Mary Anne is able to ponder over her friend Sawyer as she taps into and telepathically scans to the last point in time that Sawyer was asking questions and/or leaving impressions for her psyche to attune to.

She is then able to assimilate the information and communicate with Sawyer at that precise point in time. This is possible since the impressions were sent out into the ether waves by Sawyer to Mary Anne.

Mary Anne and Sawyer are able to interact even though Sawyer had been transmitting his thoughts to Mary Anne at a different time. Or, rather, it seemed as if it were at a different time... truly difficult to describe the exact details in words... truly difficult to comprehend through a conscious, mortal mind...

This process is similar to Mary Anne mentally scanning, or rewinding, a tape recorder to get a point in the tape where Sawyer is asking her questions and/or thinking of her. Even though Sawyer's thoughts may have already taken place previously, Mary Anne is able to communicate with those thoughts, presently, as though it were happening now. This is because; "time" operates differently in the Higher Realm than it does in the "Three Dimensional Earth Plane".

"I feel your presence, Sawyer. I am attuned to your consciousness," Mary Anne proclaimed.

"You are becoming audible to me Mary Anne." Sawyer responded, "I sense your vibrations." Mary Anne remained transfixed in her *STILL STATE* as the impressions of Sawyer solidified in her mind.

It is though time is being bent... it is as if Mary Anne is mentally traveling through a holographic field of images and she is able to see into the Past, Present and Future of her friend Sawyer.

As the extrasensory communication between Mary Anne and Sawyer coalesced, she began to hear the thoughts of Sawyer as well as envision him as he lay in his bed, asleep, in the "Three Dimensional Earth Plane".

"I can barely see you, Sawyer." Mary Anne marveled at the wondrous occurrence that was transpiring.

"*A-u-m-m-m-m-m-m-m...   A-u-m-m-m-m-m-m-m...*" she chanted, to raise the vibration of the ethereal waves around her.

This is a necessary procedure -- not simply a mere ritual -- to help aid in bringing about the proper conditions which will enable Mary Anne to communicate with Sawyer.

Marcus remained transfixed in his *state of stillness* with his thoughts focused on Christopher.

The atmosphere is filled with harmonic tones that enhance the chanting sounds that Marcus is making.

"*A-u-m-m-m-m-m-m-m... A-u-m-m-m-m-m-m-m...*"

The strong smell of myrrh permeates throughout the blissful surroundings.

Marcus' golden aura intensified with each deep breath that he drew as he continued to focus on the spirit of his friend Christopher.

"*A-u-m-m-m-m-m-m-m... A-u-m-m-m-m-m-m-m...*"

"I am with you Marcus. I have always been with you, my dear friend." The subtle tone of voice from Christopher resonated from within the consciousness of Marcus.

Marcus is euphoric. He gasped with delight at the sound of his beloved friend's voice.

"Christopher! Good God in Heavens, is that you?"

"Remain *STILL* Marcus, it is I, Christopher. I bid you greetings," Christopher continued.

"Listen to the harmonic tones as you chant, Marcus."

"*A-u-m-m-m-m-m-m-m...   A-u-m-m-m-m-m-m-m... A-u-m-m-m-m-m-m-m...   A-u-m-m-m-m-m-m-m...*" Marcus chanted.

By this time, not only is Marcus getting audible messages and impressions from Christopher; Mary Anne and Sawyer are receiving Christopher's instructions as well.

"I come to you with the Love and Light that surrounds you... the Love and Light that is within you... Mary Anne! Marcus! Sawyer! I ask that you be constant with your chanting as you focus on the harmonic tones that are emanating around you."

By now, all four beings from three dimensions are systematically, involuntarily, synchronizing themselves with one another. They become charged and united in ways that are indescribable in words.

"*A-u-m-m-m-m-m-m-m... A-u-m-m-m-m-m-m-m... A-u-m-m-m-m-m-m-m...   A-u-m-m-m-m-m-m-m...*"

"Feel the glowing white light that is embracing you... feel the Love that surrounds you..." Christopher continued.

Marcus is simply gleaming from ear to ear with the presence of his beloved friend Christopher. The two had said their farewell's to one another shortly after they had crossed over from the "Three Dimensional Earth Plane" after perishing in the house fire together.

At that time, Christopher had ascended to a Higher Dimension while Marcus remained in the Astral Plane where he has resided ever since.

Now, seemingly, like magic, Christopher was conversing with Marcus... to his delight.

"At the count of three, I want each of you to begin to slowly open up your eyes," Christopher instructed them.

"*ONE* -- continue chanting as you come up from your state of stillness. *TWO* – A-u-*m-m-m-m-m-m-m*... *A-u-m-m-m-m-m-m-m*..." Christopher chanted in accord.

"*THREE* -- open your eyes as you remain calm and relaxed."

As eyes were opened, the glorious amalgamation of three diverse realms came together as One.

Fifteen feet away, forming a triangle with Mary Anne and Marcus, stood Christopher. His golden-white aura sent shafts of illuminating light several feet out from his body.

Christopher looked very much the same as when Marcus had last seen him, with the exception of his attire.

He was wearing a brilliant yellow cloak or so it seemed. The way it blended with his aura it was difficult to discern.

Mary Anne and Marcus remained seated in a lotus position by the brook where they had been meditating.

Sawyer was not absent from this assembly. He was positioned in the middle of the triangle that was formed between the other three entities.

Although Sawyer could be seen, there was a difference in his appearance that was unique from the others. What was being viewed, by the other three, was Sawyer's Astral Body. His Physical Body was still home in his bed in the "Three Dimensional Earth Plane".

"Oh, for goodness sake's," Sawyer uttered, softly, "If I didn't know better, I would say I am having an *Out-Of-Body* experience... this is absolutely remarkable!"

"That would be my guess, too," Mary Anne pointed out.

She greeted her Earthly friend with a smile while

coming to her feet.

"It is so nice to see you, Sawyer, I can tell by the energy surrounding your body that you are still connected to the Earth Plane. My good man... you are not the first Soul, still of the flesh, that I have encountered since I made my transition to this Plane," Marcus said before crying out to the group; *"THY WILL BE DONE, ON EARTH AS IT IS IN HEAVEN."*

All four Immortals stood in awe of the strong bond that they felt toward one another during this seemingly miraculous gathering.

Keep in mind that although Sawyer still has a mortal body that is asleep in his bed back in the Earth Plane, he is also an Immortal.

Although, the "Three Dimensional Earth Plane" is a denser Plane of existence, its inhabitants are still Eternal Beings.

"Marcus, my good, good friend, as I told you when we were last together in the valley, 'There are higher worlds, as there are lower worlds'... You do remember our last time together I am quite sure?" Christopher asked.

"I remember everything that you told me. Very, very well, indeed... right up to watching you vanish before my eyes." Marcus went on and said, "For a while, I thought that I would never see you again. Recently, during my meditations, I began to sense that I would be seeing you... I began to sense that I was in contact with you..." Marcus explained.

Several white doves flew low in the sky with one of them landing on Christopher's hand as he extended his arm toward it.

The two looked each other in the eyes as Christopher smiled while gently thrusting his arm upward to send the beautiful white dove on its way again.

The four Immortals walked closer to one another in order to become better acquainted.

Christopher and Marcus, now face to face, gave each other a warm and loving embrace.

Mary Anne moved toward Sawyer as she held up her arms with the palms of her hands facing toward him.

Gloriously, she sent shafts of brilliant pink light in his

direction. This was an act of Love which could be felt by Sawyer as it encompassed his total vibratory field which was surrounding him.

Sawyer drew a deep breath, holding it for several seconds and then released it slowly out of his mouth as he instinctively reciprocated with a thrilling manifestation and display of luminosity. He stood, mesmerized, as he witnessed his own ability to direct *Loving Energy* in the form of pink beams of beautiful light toward Mary Anne.

All of the sudden, at one wave of Christopher's hand, the four Immortals were no longer standing by the brook.

A bewildered Marcus cried out, "What happened? Where are we?"

"We truly do create our reality, Marcus. Some of us are better at it then others." Christopher winked at Marcus as he put on one of his big smiles that Marcus was oh, so, familiar with.

Sawyer spoke up before being interrupted, "This is either one magnificent dream or else..."

"There is no cause for alarm my friend. You are *Out-Of-Body* and will be awakening from your bed in due time," Christopher assured the young man.

"I have brought you all to yet a Higher Realm in *Collective Consciousness* so that you can witness where I often frequent when I 'take-on' a human form or a 'desire-body'."

The surroundings seemed a bit more surreal and lighter to that of the place where Mary Anne and Marcus dwelled.

The four appeared to be standing on snow-white, glistening sand where there were soft foamy waves splashing to the shore just ahead of them.

"There are many realms within the Astral Realm... this is one of them," Christopher explained.

"Where is the Sphere? I do not see the Sphere?" Mary Anne asked, noticing that the Sphere that she often meditated to was not in the sky.

The sky had a stunning golden radiance to it with oscillating clouds of various shapes and colors.

"You are standing in it," Christopher grinned, with a sparkle in his eyes that reassured the bemused Mary Anne.

"You see, my friends, some things are not always as they appear. What you thought was an object was really just an idea," Christopher explained.

He continued, "The Sphere, in the sky, far away, represents something greater... something beyond one's understanding... something unknown."

Christopher pointed toward the Heavens.

"Thinking makes it so. He repeated, "Thinking makes it so."

Christopher began to chant. "Listen to the tones. Listen to the harmony all around you."

The tranquil sounds of music were filling the air.

To the group's amazement they watched a new Sphere being formed in the sky merely by Christopher's strong will and desire to create it.

It started to take shape and form as a vaporous like cloud that was violet blue in color with a tint of red around it.

"There, now! I think you get the idea." Christopher ended his concentration on the development of the Sphere while he continued to speak.

"Keep in mind that the Sphere I just created for you is an example of what the thoughts from one Immortal can do if One's desire is strong enough."

The three Immortals listened attentively while Christopher continued to ramble on.

"Although it may be difficult at this time for you to understand; remember that your past is being recreated by your future thoughts just as your future is being created by your present thoughts... as you continue to develop in consciousness along your transcendental path you uplift those in your past, present and future, thereby altering it... actually, in true-reality, the past and future are so intertwined with the present that they only appear to be separate... there are no limits except those that you place on yourself... in the ultimate Reality, the *Eternal Now* is all that there is."

Sawyer blurted out, "Home is where the heart is. This is marvelous here. I absolutely love it!"

"Yes it is 'marvelous here' my good fellow. You have work to do on Earth. But, you will return to this Realm when it is time," Christopher said with a joyful look upon his face.

The four Immortals continued to remain in this

superlative land as they conversed and walked along the seashore.

"It is very serene here by the water," Mary Anne observed.

Christopher remarked, "This is my world... my creation so to speak. I descend to here, or come down to *this place* when I wish to manifest and take on form... you see, my friends, there are many levels of consciousness... many levels of existence... we can all take a seat up ahead on those rocks and watch the waves for a spell," Christopher suggested to his friends.

The four made there way over to a small sea cliff to rest and listen to Christopher shed light on some complex truths.

"Within the Astral Plane there are many levels or layers. You are in what I would call the very Highest Levels of this so-called Plane of existence," Christopher stated.

"It does seem a little lighter up here," Marcus chuckled as he looked toward Christopher.

"I am pleased that you brought your sense of humor with you, Marcus."

"Now, as I was saying, we are very close to the next dimension... I am not referring to the 'Three Dimensional Earth Plane', when I say this... I come here when I manifest. I spend much of my *'time'* outside, or beyond, the limits of *'time'* within a Higher Plane of Existence whereby I am in a state of deep meditative bliss. I go beyond shape and form... I become an observer of *'All That There Is'*." Christopher continued rambling on as his friends listened inventively.

"The Sphere that we are in, this moment in time, in True Reality, is not literally a Sphere at all. Rather, it is an *'idea'* of a Sphere, as is the one that I created a little while ago... at times; our minds need to envision these meaningful illusions in order to grow beyond our current states of consciousness. Do you follow what I am proposing to you?"

Sawyer spoke up at this time and asked, "Are your observations and mediations witnessed and conducted by yourself; or, are there others with you throughout your experiences?"

"I slip into a *'Collective Consciousness'* whereby, I am 'One' with others and others are 'One' with me... there are no words to fully explain the natural phenomenon that I am referring to, other than to say that I become Omnificent."

Mary Anne added her opinion, "The way a mortal sheds his physical body and moves on to the Astral Plane; you dissolve your Astral Body and merge with *THE SOURCE*. Our ultimate *HOME...* You *FIND YOUR WAY HOME...*" she concluded with a shimmer of satisfaction on her smiling face.

"Yes my dear, that is very astute and well put. Thank you. In so many words; I take my Luminous Body and I venture inward beyond any limits of the imagination," Christopher said.

"You have me thinking so much, now. This is like 'old times'... there is so much I want to ask you," Marcus said.

"Take with you what I have said and settle for that at this time," Christopher suggested. "Take a deep breath and look at this beautiful, tranquil sea. Look how gentle the waves splash against the rocks... It is truly a wonderland to give thanks for," Christopher remarked.

Many unanswered truths were revealed to Mary Anne, Marcus and Sawyer. They were informed by Christopher that much of what was being told to them would remain deep-rooted in their Higher Consciousness although a great deal of what was being conveyed would not be retained on a conscious level when they departed this Realm.

They were reassured that they could return to this *Place* again at some other point in time.

"Farewells are necessary in order for reunions to take place," Christopher imparted.

Marcus looked toward his friend, sensing that their visit with Christopher was coming to an end.

"No need to be upset, Marcus. Our time has come, as it has gone, once again, my dear friend," Christopher stated while announcing the time had, indeed, arrived for the three Immortals to return to their respective Realms.

Christopher was vibrating at a higher frequency then the other three Immortals.

His golden-white aura had increased in diameter and was now extending out about six feet from his body in a display of shimmering beams of light.

"Continue your work as a Dharmacist... enjoy your labor of love in your 'world'... in your Realm..." Christopher said to his friend, Marcus.

"Mary Anne, it was my ultimate pleasure to meet you and become briefly acquainted. And, yours as well, Sawyer... the work that you two are doing together, as you help build a bridge between two worlds, is of the utmost importance. As the consciousness of mankind continues to unfold they shall realize the magnitude and purpose of their existence within their dimension... keep going forward with your work... both of you," Christopher said.

"Thank you, we will," the two responded as Mary Anne returned the compliment with her soft smile. "We will indeed."

Sawyer spoke out with emotion. "I am honored to have met all of you."

Christopher gave a penetrating look that was almost hypnotic, directly into the eyes of Sawyer, as he said, "Hand down my message to the troubled Souls on Earth. When the time is right for you, be sure and tell them that *THE SOURCE* dwells deep within each of their Souls. *THE SOURCE* dwells deep within you."

"Ah, I will, Sir. I most definitely will," Sawyer promised, a bit surprised by the profound command.

Christopher, then, looked out into the waters. He informed his Immortal friends to cast any uncertainties that they may have into the Sea so that they may be dissolved.

The Immortals took a few moments to give thanks for the wonderful visit to the Realm.

"So, to use your words, my beloved Marcus, 'We will meet again. We will meet again'," Christopher declared as he prepared the three Immortals for their departure.

Marcus gave special thanks for his reunion with his teacher and friend as he hugged Christopher goodbye.

"I want you all to say the words; *I AM STILL...*"

The spellbinding, guided meditation continued until both Mary Anne and Marcus where coming out of their meditations by the brook where they had began and Sawyer was back in his Physical Body at home in his bed, fast asleep.

Sawyer slowly awakened from his so-called *'dream state'*. To be more to the point, his Astral Body had re-entered his Physical Body and the two bodies where now in sync as one body. Sawyer was gradually returning to his fully conscious state of awareness.

Sawyer sat up in bed as he glanced at the large, beautiful picture on his wall. It was an inspiring acrylic painting that was done by a very close friend of his and given to him as a gift. The Heavenly picture came complete with Angels, a couple of unicorns and a wizard in a purple robe wearing a matching colored coned hat with white stars on it.

Sawyer thought aloud, "Oh my God, that was an unbelievable journey that I just had. It was as surreal as this picture. I have to write this down." Sawyer grabbed his pen and black leather journal that he kept by the bedside table for writing down notes for times such as this.

1. I left my body…

2. I met Mary Anne…

3. I met her husband, Marcus.

4. I met this advanced being, Christopher, from a Higher Realm.

5. I left my body and 'Astrally' traveled to Mary Anne's Realm and then went on to a Higher Realm as well.

Sawyer quickly jotted down some notes in an effort to encapsulate his fascinating *Out-Of-Body* experience. He then set down his journal as he got up to walk over to look out the window in his bedroom.

"Our Creator surely does have a plan for each and every one of us," he thought to himself, as he looked down at the stream of traffic outside his twelfth floor Condominium where the Sun was just beginning to show its face.

"Look at all of those people running off to work so early in the morning. Everyone with different goals… different dreams… we cannot always see it, but we are all part of the *'Whole'*. We are all connected."

Validations were coming to Sawyer's mind -- a sense of knowing -- as he continued to put into perspective the incredible *Out-Of-Body* journey that had recently occurred.

The memories were still solidifying in his mind.

"P u r r r r r r r r r r... Meow..." A deep rumbled purring sound could be heard in the room as Sawyer's pretty Maine Coon Cat came up and nudged its head against the calf of his leg.

"Well, hello to you too, Fluffy," Sawyer returned the greeting while picking up his adorable long-haired, gray and white companion.

"I know, I know, it is your mealtime... in a minute, just hold on for a moment," Sawyer informed his cat, Fluffy.

"Life is good. Life is truly good."

AND TIME ROLLED ON

Back at the brook, Mary Anne and Marcus composed themselves. Regaining their normal sense of awareness, they were not quite sure what had transpired. Yet both were fully aware that they had gone deep into a selected Meditation and had visited with Christopher and Sawyer.

Suffice it to say, they had successfully made personal contact with two other Realms simultaneously. Marcus raised himself up from his lotus position and then walked over to his wife to help her up to her feet.

"I must say that was utterly fascinating. I am still beside myself with all that occurred," Marcus commented to his wife.

"Give me a moment, please," Mary Anne requested.

Mary Anne turned and looked at the undulating brook. She, then, noticed a small bridge that was downstream about ten or fifteen yards away.

She turned back toward her husband, "Let's walk down over there, Marcus. I would like to walk a bit," she emphasized to Marcus while reaching out to join hands with him.

"All right, my dear," Marcus concurred while taking his wife's hand, "All right."

"We Bi-located, I am convinced of it!" Mary Anne blurted out, "We both remained here by the brook in our *STILL STATE.* Yet, at the same time, we walked in a Higher Realm with your friend Christopher and my Earthly friend, Sawyer."

"I have to think about this a moment, dear," Marcus responded, still somewhat in awe of what had transpired.

"As incredible as it may sound, we surmounted one Realm and yet we never left it." Mary Anne became increasingly convinced of her theory.

Marcus came to a halt as the couple approached the bridge that was suspended over the brook. With his eyebrows raised in his trademarked fashion Marcus succumbed to Mary Anne's hypothesis.

"I never would have looked at it that way, my dear, but I have to agree with you on this. We were engrossed in our *STILL STATE*... we were sitting down by the brook... yet, we did visit Christopher... and we visited him up in that Sphere," Marcus avowed while pointing up toward the glowing Sphere, "We did indeed."

Mary Anne went on, "It is actually quite simple. All we did was what Sawyer did... we remained in one dimension while traveling to another one." She let out a delightful sigh of relief after having assimilated their recent journey.

"... A-u-m-m-m-m-m-m-m... 'Shanti, Shanti,' Peace, Peace," Mary Anne affirmed aloud, while holding up her arms and extending her the palms of her hands out to the illuminating sky.

Just then, a fine-looking specimen of a white dove swirled down from above as Marcus extended his hand to welcome it. The beautiful bird settled on Marcus' arm.

"Perhaps it is a symbol?" Mary Anne questioned what was happening, "Maybe it is a confirmation that we did indeed transcend our Realm," she said.

Marcus gently stroked the soft dove with his index finger from the nape of its neck to just above its tail. The shimmering white dove let out a couple of coos and then flew off on its way.

"Perhaps it is. Like the old saying goes; 'As Above, So Below'," Marcus said.

"Marcus, do you recall how difficult it is when you attempt to Astral Travel back to the Earth Plane?"

"Yes, it is so dense that one has a grueling time traveling there. It is like cutting your way through a jungle or something..." Marcus remarked.

Mary Anne glanced down into the brook for a moment and then said, "I think that it works the same way in reverse. I think that we had a unique experience being able to travel up to Christopher's Realm within that Sphere. I, also, believe that we may have visited that Sphere one other time... when we had our 'Group Med' with Shirley and Clark."

Marcus could tell that his wife was still very excited from their recent journey.

"We are blessed, Mary Anne." Marcus reached over and gave his wife a big hug and a little kiss on her lips.

Pink shafts of light were emanating several feet out from the auras of Mary Anne and Marcus. The love that they both had for one another was immeasurable.

"I love you, Mary Anne."

"And, I love you, too Marcus. I love you forever and then some."

The two Soul-Mates resumed their walk and headed over the "little bridge" failing to notice an additional "symbol" of the amazing experience they had undergone together.

AND TIME ROLLED ON

"You are up and ready I see." Marcus said to his wife while slowly awakening from a deep and restful sleep.

"Yes I am, dear. I have been walking in the flower garden. It is so beautiful out there. I absolutely adore our garden, Marcus. Are you renewed enough to go to school now or would you like to remain here for a bit? Would you like some refreshment?"

"No, that is quite alright. My class awaits me. I am ready," Marcus said as held his head back, moving it from side to side, while becoming fully alert.

"Would you like to take the 'fast' way to school?"

"Why not, Mary Anne, let's do. We must not keep our students waiting," Marcus responded.

Mary Anne went over and sat next to Marcus on the soft cushions.

"Take my hand. Envision the side of Everest Hall, near the fountain, Marcus."

Marcus took hold of Mary Anne and together they closed their eyes and focused on being present at Everest Hall, as suggested.

"I AM AT EVEREST HALL. I AM AT EVEREST HALL," the two willed aloud.

Both, Mary Anne and Marcus could hear swooshing sounds as they experienced the feeling of being hurled through Inner Space.

Seemingly, in an instant, both were relocated from their abode and opening their eyes at the College on the side of Everest Hall. They are now standing by a small running fountain which is situated in the middle of some hedges.

"Well, my dear, I shall see you after class, then, all right?" she said.

Marcus gave his wife a loving hug and gentle kiss, "Yes, after class... Actually, I will see you back at our abode. I am going to walk a bit when I get through here," Marcus said. He added, "Go in *good spirits* my dear."

The two departed and were off to their designated

classes. While on his way down the hall to begin his class, Marcus peeked into a doorway to view what was taking place in another Dharmacist's classroom. It was a class of approximately one hundred-fifty pupils.

The Teacher, who went by the name, Hanna, was a vision of beauty to behold.

Her shimmering aura had a golden glow about it that seemed to sparkle as she moved. This aura extended out from her body further than that of nearly everyone else that was present in the classroom.

Hanna was formally of another country, other than the one that most of the students were from. This was no problem, being able to understand Hanna, on the part of the students.

What is so wonderful in the Higher Realm is the ability for the Immortals to comprehend one another in spite of the fact that they may have come from different countries where its inhabitants speak other languages. This extraordinary ability is but one of many that the Immortals possess within the Higher Realms. There are many Immortals from different regions, within the Higher Realms, that speak a variety of languages. Some of these Immortals have never chosen to incarnate into the "Three Dimensional Earth Plane" and yet communication is transmitted from Immortal to Immortal in the language that the Immortal is familiar in hearing. This is due to the fact that speaking in the Higher Realm is actually the manifestation of the entities thought which comes out in a vibratory tone and is systematically translated to the listener by method of natural law.

Marcus nodded to his counterpart who was speaking to a classroom full of students on the "Tools of Time".

Marcus listened thoroughly for a moment on what the Teacher was saying;

"When attempting to measure or envision what 'time' is like in the Higher Realms, from within the scope of the 'Three Dimensional Earth Plane', or, what 'time' is like within the 'Three Dimensional Earth Plane' from within the scope of the Higher Realms, it can truly seem like a paradox from either standpoint.

When viewed from the Astral Realm, a mortal's entire life, on the Earth Plane, can seem like a 'blink of an eye' or on 'fast speed' – passing by very quickly; or it can seem like merely a week, or a month. Perceptions of 'time' will always vary according to circumstances.

An entity, while focused on his or her incarnation within the 'Three Dimensional Earth Plane', can accomplish a great deal and learn valuable lessons.

It boggles the mind to attempt to comprehend the vast differences of the utilization of 'time' from Realm to Realm.

A simple way to explain this so-called 'time' difference is that it is immeasurable and there is a dissimilarity that cannot be put into words... In true reality, 'time' is but an illusion.

Only, until you step outside the boundaries of 'time' can you truly understand the 'Divine Laws' that govern it. Even then it is too great a challenge for most entities and the variables are immense."

After digesting a bit of what the Teacher was discussing with regard to the "Tools of Time", Marcus waved farewell to Hanna, the Dharmacist, and continued on his path.

The hallway was filled with New Souls and Old Souls that were coming and going to their various classes in search of understanding, meaning and a sense of purpose and fulfillment.

Marcus entered his classroom where his students were eagerly awaiting his arrival.

"I bid you a fond 'Good Day'," Marcus greeted his class. "It is wonderful to be here."

"Hello."

"Good Day."

"Good Day."

The students welcomed Marcus to the classroom.

Marcus sat back on the edge of his desk as he began speaking to his class.

"I can see that our class is continually growing. Therefore, we will not go through with the formality of a Roll

Call. There are no grades here, as you know, except for the ones that you give yourself," Marcus reminded his class.

"All right, let us begin, shall we? As all of you know my vocation while on Earth was that of a Minster. In addition to Preaching to my Congregation I was in continuous search of the Truth... of what Life was all about. I guess one could say that I was 'Soul-Searching'." Marcus stood up while he continued speaking.

"It wasn't until later in my life -- after I had lost my wife and had retired -- that I finally gained a better understanding and insight into what my Ministry had truly meant to me." Marcus slowly paced, from one side of the room to the other, as he explained some of his past to the class.

"You see, in my early days on Earth, I was taught to look outward for God... I envisioned our Creator as though he was a 'He' and was anthropomorphic."

"What does that mean? 'A-n-t-h-r-o-p-o-m-o-r,' I cannot even pronounce it," Jason laughed while asking his question.

"Quite simply, it means that I personalized THE SOURCE from which we all stem." Marcus responded to Jason before continuing on.

"In my particular Religion, as a Christian, I was taught that 'Jesus of Nazareth' was the 'Son of God' and that everyone on Earth was a sinner. I was taught to belittle myself and be ashamed of who I was, in so many ways... I do not believe that was the Great Master Teacher Jesus' message at all. I finally concluded after a long period of 'time' that 'Jesus of Nazareth's' message was that a small nucleus inside of us is, in fact, 'Our Creator' – The Father Is Within -- and that we must cultivate and nurture this gift, from which we stem, for we would be nothing -- 'NO THING'-- without it," Marcus paused for a moment.

"As time passed, in my incarnation on Earth, I met a dear friend who I came to know, and have a great admiration and respect for, by the name of Christopher. He taught me, or should I say that he reminded me, to 'Go Inward' and realize that our Creator, or, THE SOURCE, is inside each and everyone of us -- as it was in 'Jesus of Nazareth' – and that it is our 'birthright', so-to-speak, to claim and to recognize this 'Energy Source', from which we all stem, is inside of us all," Marcus was rambling.

The class remained transfixed as Marcus shared his heartfelt story with them. Except for the sound of Marcus' voice, the room was totally silent as he picked up a crystal ball from his desk and began gazing into it.

"What do you see in there?" asked Jason. He was not being rude. He simply could not resist posing the silly question to his Teacher.

Marcus laughed as he momentarily held the crystal ball down by his side and then held it back up to explain, "The crystal ball is merely a 'tool' to aid me in clarifying my thoughts. You ought to try it some time, Jason." Marcus smiled at the class and continued speaking, gazing at the crystal ball for a few moments and then placing it back down on the desk.

"The Universe fills all Space, inner and outer, invisible and visible; and is nearing the end of 'The Piscean Age' as it sits on the cusp of 'The Aquarian Age'. Mortal men and women, as well as Immortals such as ourselves, are becoming awakened more and more each and every day to the glorious self-realization that *THE SOURCE* dwells deep in the abyss of each and every one of us..." Marcus paused a moment as he scanned the roomful of students.

"I don't think I ever mentioned to you how I met my physical demise on the Earth Plane. My dear friend, Christopher, and I perished in a house fire together... after we had crossed over to this dimension his last words to me – before he went on to a Higher Realm – were..." Marcus paused to draw his breath while coming to halt in the center of the front of the room as he looked at his students.

"MAY GOD IN YOU SHINE THROUGH. Let me repeat those six words to you, once again, because they are very important," Marcus raised his arms as he spoke.

He reiterated as he continued with his compelling story, "MAY GOD IN YOU SHINE THROUGH."

"I have attempted to become a divine servant as

well as a proud Master of those six words... for one to recognize, what some of you refer to as God and others refer to as *THE SOURCE*, that this Divine Energy is not separate from us... is not 'outside' of us... but, rather, is 'inside' of us... to repeat; *THE SOURCE* 'dwells deep in the abyss of each and every one of us'... to come to this self-realization is what all of the Great Master Teachers, through the annals of time, have attempted to enlighten us with, in so many words." Marcus leaned back against his desk as he continued to observe his classroom of students.

Marcus was exerting a great deal of energy as he shared his thoughts with the class. The deep-dark salmon part of his aura remained in place while the sunny yellow and geranium purple outer bands expanded, pulsating rapidly.

"I realize that some of my classes tend to be more of a sermon, or a speech, rather than a 'class'. Often, this is a good way to learn," Marcus said.

"I found your story very enlightening," a student cried out from the back of the room.

"I extend to you the opportunity to ask me any questions that you may have at this time."

"'MAY GOD IN YOU SHINE THROUGH.' I like that very much. We are all composed of Divine Energy... of the Life Force... of the God Force. It is a matter of becoming aware of it... becoming attuned to it," Amethyst remarked in a soft-spoken voice.

The class continued for a while longer as students interacted with one another and discussed the concept of their connection to *THE SOURCE*.

The Immortals were in harmony and at peace with each other. You could see, hear and feel the love that was made manifest in the room. All was calm... all was good...

In Mary Anne's "Mediumship Communication" class, the gigantic oval shaped, silvery metallic, screen was pulsating, within its own parameter, as her students directed their messages for their loved ones upon it.

Thanks to Mary Anne's profound channeling abilities, she and her pupils are once again able to view what is taking place in Sawyer's classroom in the "Three Dimensional Earth Plane".

Due to popular demand, Mary Anne's sessions were evolving more into conveying messages to loved ones in the "Three Dimensional Earth Plane" and less in the actual teachings of "Mediumship." However, she made sure that all of her students learned how to make use of the "Light" by envisioning pure white light around their loves ones in the "Three Dimensional Earth Plane".

Meanwhile, Sawyer is receiving telepathic impressions from Mary Anne and her classroom of students. He processes and then transmits the information to his audience that is seated around him in the prearranged circle that has been formed.

Currently, Sawyer's "Spiritual Reunion" classes last for about an hour. While he spends considerable time delivering messages from the loved ones of the people in his class; Sawyer also takes the opportunity to remind his scholars of the great importance and significance of their presence in their current dimension.

Sawyer was picking up thoughts at random from Mary Anne's class.

He said, as he turned toward the general direction of a gentleman that was seated several rows back in the audience, "I sense a female vibration coming forward by the name of Clarice or Clarissa."

"My wife's name is Clarissa," the gentleman attested in a somewhat nervous tone of voice.

"Yes, that is the one," Sawyer responded.

"Did you have a picture that was in your house... a picture that your wife liked... you didn't like... a picture of a horse... a horse's head or something?" Sawyer was doing his best to relay the information as he received it.

"Yes, I..."

"Just say Yes or No. Sometimes when you offer too much information it distracts from what is being transmitted to me," Sawyer interrupted the fellow to explain.

"Yes," the man minimized his response to a word.

Sawyer placed his hand on his chin as he stepped from side to side while deciphering the rest of the message.

"Well, Clarissa wants to let you know that she is not upset with you for giving away that picture. She forgives the incident," Sawyer responded with amusement.

The crowd laughed at the humorous message that was being delivered.

"Does this make sense?" Sawyer asked.

"Yes it does indeed. Can I explain about the picture?" The man was grinning.

"Sure. Let us in on it," Sawyer gestured with a smile.

"I used to joke with Clarissa that if she 'went' before I did that I was going to throw that darn picture away... I gave it away instead."

"Well, sir, this is her way of letting you know that she is aware of what you did and that she is not upset about the incident." Sawyer assured the man as he moved on to another message, "It is her way of affirming to you that everything is okay."

Sawyer turned to his right and looked into the audience.

"I have someone here who had some kind of Pulmonary Disease. I feel a shortness in breath... it is a male vibration. He was from Scotland," Sawyer explained.

"My husband was from Scotland."

"Did he have some sort of problem with breathing?" Sawyer asked.

"Not that I am aware of," she replied.

"No, no... It's not coming from over here," Sawyer turned around and faced the portion of the audience that was seated behind him.

"Who had serious problems with their breathing? They may have even 'crossed over' with this ailment... I am getting a name like; Gordy or Gordon?"

"My brother's name was Gordon. We called him 'Gordy'," an elderly woman, who was seated toward the back of the room, spoke up.

"Yes, the message is for you."

Sawyer then asked, "He had difficulties with his breathing, correct?"

"He had Emphysema. He passed away over fifteen years ago. We called him 'Gordy' when he was a teenager," the woman hurriedly explained before Sawyer could limit her response to a brief confirmation.

"Well, he is here and wants to let you know that, although his crossing over into the next dimension was difficult, everything is okay." Sawyer delivered the reassuring message to the woman.

"He used to smoke that pipe all day long," she added while shaking her head displeasingly.

Sawyer finished with his message, "He sends his blessings of love to you this day."

"I thank you," she said.

"For those of you here today that were unable to receive a message from your loved ones; do not fret. The important, main message to note is that life goes on, beyond the 'Physical Dimension'." Sawyer turned slowly in order to address everyone in the circle of people that were present. "It would be a good idea to remember to think of your loved ones in the next dimension often, and to send them loving thoughts."

He continued, "When you picture the likeness of your loved ones, place an imaginary pink or white light around their image. Encompass their total being with this loving light... for that matter, it is also a good idea to place this light around your own aura when mentally envisioning yourselves," Sawyer took a moment to ensure that his audience was digesting his proposals.

"White light is for protection and healing. Pink light is for Love." Sawyer urged his students, "Keep working with the light."

"Love, Love, Love. Love is all you need," Sawyer smiled, as he sang part of the lyrics to an old "Beatles" song, written by John Lennon and Paul McCartney, titled, "All You Need Is Love."

The auras from the people in Sawyer's audience seemed to exude a vibrant glow as their energies were uplifted by their inspiring session with one another.

Over in the next dimension, Mary Anne's class was winding down. It had been a fruitful gathering and many messages had been delivered from Mary Anne's group of students to Sawyer's class in the "Three Dimensional Earth Plane".

Mary Anne's students seemed to be invigorated to have partaken in the exchange between the two worlds.

AND TIME ROLLED ON

The sound of a dog barking could be heard in the distance as Marcus began to awaken from a deep and restful sleep.

Shelby was eagerly waiting for Mary Anne to throw the ball for him to chase one more time.

"Run and fetch it, Shelby," Mary Anne said.

With a glow in his eyes of sheer delight, Shelby ran after the bright yellow ball.

"Hurry up," she added.

Shelby gently took hold of the ball. He lifted his head up toward the sky while shaking it from side to side as his ears flapped due to the momentum of it all.

"Good boy. Oh, what a good boy. Now bring it back," she said, like she did so often when Shelby came to visit. Mary Anne and her four-legged friend were having a grand time together.

Still gathering his senses, Marcus emerged from the house and meandered into the meadow following the sounds of his wife and Shelby.

"Mary Anne. There you are," Marcus said.

Shelby came running over to greet Marcus. He attempted to jump up and place his two front paws on Marcus' stomach but Marcus held up his right arm and kindly discouraged the dog's intention.

"Hello Shelby," Marcus said while patting him on the head.

"Did you have a good rest, Marcus?" asked Mary Anne.

"Yes I did... well, yes and no, actually," Marcus responded with a concerned look upon his face.

He continued, "I had another vivid dream concerning Robert. It was almost as if I were there... perhaps I was there... although, Robert was not aware of my presence to 'his world'. I want to go back and visit him and make my presence known... I desire to speak with him." Marcus was eager.

"Our son, Robert...?" Mary Anne asked.

"Yes. Yes, Robert," Marcus repeated.

After Mary Anne's departure from the "Three

Dimensional Earth Plane" Robert had become increasingly disillusioned and estranged from his father, Marcus.

Robert eventually rebelled against his father's religious beliefs and philosophies. He had slowly turned into a sort of atheist, rejecting any beliefs that he once held of a higher power or eternal life.

Robert had spent the rest of his years on Earth obsessed in making money. He neglected to take time out for friends and what few relatives were left.

Actually, Robert neglected to take much time out for anything, having lost any meaningful purpose in life other than to generate cash from his Real Estate Developing firm.

The day finally came when Robert made his transition from the "Three Dimensional Earth Plane" to the Astral Realm, several years after the death of his father.

Robert was in his sixties at the time of his passing from a heart condition that was bought on by bitterness and stress. He had been well received by his parents, upon his so-called death, when he crossed over into their dimension. Both were there to greet their son with loving arms when Robert's "energy" appeared to them.

However, due to a different level of consciousness, Robert was unable to sustain in the Realm that his parents were in and soon drifted into his own world.

Although, Robert's world is still far above what would be referred to as the Lower Realms of existence; it is nevertheless much more confining, dreary and isolated then that of the Higher Realms where Mary Anne and Marcus reside.

All that Mary Anne and Marcus could do -- up until Marcus' recent vision -- was to envision pink lights and white lights around Robert as they prayed for his peace of mind.

"Well, I am going with you then. I would like to see Robert too," Mary Anne said in a concerned voice.

"I feel that I need to speak with him alone. I had a strong vision, I tell you. We need to resolve some issues that we have with one another. This has become clear to me. Furthermore, it may not be an easy journey going to see him," Marcus surmised.

"Marcus, dear, you can speak with him alone. But, I am going with you." Mary Anne was steadfast.

"Very well,   we will go and see Robert together," Marcus consented.

"Ruff, Ruff." Shelby barked.

"No, Shelby," Mary Anne replied with a chuckle, "You are staying here in the meadow."

Marcus laughed out loud.

Mary Anne picked up the yellow ball and threw it out into the field one more time for Shelby. He ran speedily and retrieved the ball.

"Good boy. You run along now Shelby. We shall meet again," Mary Anne said.

"Yes, off you go, Shelby. We love you," Marcus said as he turned and reached over to Mary Anne to join arms.

Shelby ran off into the meadow, quite contented to romp and play.

"First some refreshment, and then we shall prepare for our journey," Marcus said to his wife.

The two smiled at one another as they headed back toward their home.

After some refreshment Mary Anne and Marcus sat down and held hands as they readied themselves to visit their son, Robert.

Mary Anne was exceptionally energized. The couple had not been in communication with their son since shortly after his crossing over into the Astral Plane. Mary Anne and Marcus had high hopes that Robert would come around eventually.

"Now, Mary Anne, I must tell you that when I viewed Robert and his surroundings they appeared to be somewhat isolated and depressing. Are you sure that you want to come with me?"

"I most definitely want to come with you. I do not want you going to Robert's 'world' by yourself. Furthermore, if there is anything I can do to help; I surely would like to be there for Robert," she convinced her husband.

"So be it," Marcus said.

Together, they closed their eyes and went into a quick *STILL STATE* of awareness as they had both become quite adept in going into the *STILL STATE.*

They squeezed each other's hand as they said in unison, "*I AM STILL.*"

"It is our utmost desire to be with our son, Robert, at this time. We wish to join him in his 'world'," Marcus said aloud.

"*Au-m-m-m-m-m-m-m...*" Mary Anne chanted.

The chanting resonated to the center of their luminous bodies as a swooshing sound enveloped the couple. Quickly, the fantastic sensation of spiraling through Inner Space captivated the two adventurous Souls.

As the powerful sensations and swooshing sounds subsided, a sense of calmness overtook them. Mary Anne and Marcus opened their eyes to view a totally different land before them.

"Yes, this is the place," Marcus said as he took a brief look at the landscape surrounding them, "How do you feel my dear?"

"I am fine, Marcus. My word, this place is eerie, I must declare," Mary Anne uttered softly, "Will you look at these trees?"

The harmonic tones that filled the air are of a lower pitch then that of the Higher Realm where Mary Anne and Marcus reside. The colors of the land and sky are less vibrant due to a lower frequency level.

"We shall head over there," Marcus pointed toward some huge, wide stone steps that were up ahead.

They made their way to the steps leaving behind the thickly wooded area which had been their point of entry to this strange land.

The steps are not only wide from side to side, they also are long, extending outward so that the couple had to take about four or five paces before stepping down each step.

As the two made their descent down the wide stone steps they took a quick look to the left and to the right.

Mary Anne and Marcus are able to see about ten

yards in each direction before the visibility became obscured by a dense misty blue colored fog. Having traveled down about a dozen steps, Marcus motioned to his wife for them to stop for a moment.

"This is just like in the vision I had. Will you look at the interesting floral patterns within these steps?" Marcus remarked.

"The colors are rather drab. However the design resembles a Persian Carpet," Mary Anne commented.

"Yes, it does. Let us proceed, shall we? We will be there soon. We are almost half way there," Marcus assured his wife while patting her arm as a gesture of encouragement. The two continued down the wide, stone-like stairs.

What appeared to be a bleak and desolate village, positioned within a bluish-gray canyon, came into view.

"It is so gloomy here, Marcus. There is no effervescence. Where are the wondrous colors? There is no vivacity in the environment," Mary Anne declared.

"Would you like to turn back my dear?" Marcus asked with concern.

"No, of course I do not want to turn back. I am simply making an observation."

"This is just like my vision, only this time you are with me." Marcus went on explaining, "We have reached the point in which we must close our eyes, once again, and visualize being outside Robert's abode."

"We did that before," Mary Anne pointed out.

He looked Mary Anne closely in her eyes as he continued to explain, "Dear, we have descended to a lower vibratory state of existence, although we are still within the safety of the Higher Realm."

"In my earlier vision of my visit to Robert it also took two phases to get there. We are very close. Robert is a thought away at this point of the juncture," he said.

"Would you like me to close my eyes now?" Mary Anne smiled as she asked her husband for further instructions.

Marcus took hold of both his wife's hands with his hands and said, "Yes dear, I would like that."

Together, they closed their eyes and quickly went

into the *STILL STATE.*

"*I AM STILL. STILL I AM,*" Marcus said aloud.

"*A-u-m-m-m-m-m-m-m...*" Mary Anne chanted in order to raise their vibrations.

The now familiar swooshing sound came over them once again as the couple experienced the accelerated motion of traveling though Inner Space.

As the sounds and sensations subsided Mary Anne and Marcus opened their eyes to find themselves in close proximity to a small cottage that was positioned in an alcove southwest of the village.

The safe and extraordinary journey had come to an end. Mary Anne and Marcus were finally within several yards of their son Robert's place of residence.

The parents walked up to the door of the cottage, after making their way through some small weeds and brush.

Mary Anne cried out to her son, "Robert, dear, are you in there?"

"This is your father, son. I have journeyed here with your mother. Are you around?"

Robert was inside the cottage. He could hear his parents, who were just outside the door, calling to him.

This brought back an instantaneous flashback of when Robert was a small boy and his father was calling out to him. The images, of long ago, vanished rapidly as Robert regained his faculties.

"Hello! Yes, ah, come inside," Robert's startled voice cried out in response, "Yeah, this is Robert!"

Marcus gently pushed open the door to find Robert standing near a table by a small window which overlooked the mountain canyons and lots of woody scrubs.

The parents walked up to their son and together they hugged him, each placing one hand on his back and the other on his chest. Mary Anne and Marcus enveloped Robert and the entire cottage with ultra beams of pink light which they manifested by the powerful love that they had for their son.

"It is wonderful to see you. We have missed you and have thought of you often," Mary Anne assured her son.

"Yes. It is terrific to see you, Robert. I had a dream about you and me, and I wanted to convey some thoughts to you," Marcus said.

Robert's aura was short-cropped and only extended out several inches from the outline of his luminous body. The deprived aura was due to the blocked energy flow that was stemming from Robert's consciousness.

"I am happy to see you both, too. I am just bemused. You have caught me by surprise," Robert responded, a bit taken back and somewhat astonished.

Due to Robert's conception of reality and current belief-system he still maintained an appearance similar to the age that he was at the time of his crossing over from the "Three Dimensional Earth Plane". He actually looked older than his parents. His attire appeared to be the same as what he wore while on Earth.

"We have undergone quite a frequency change to be able to come here and be with you, son," said Marcus while glancing at Mary Anne.

"How did you get here? I am still a bit perplexed. How have you been? There are so many questions coming to my mind," Robert probed his father for answers, "Would you like to sit down?" he added, pointing toward another section of the room.

The three looked over at a big comfortable chair against the wall. Suddenly, the area became rather fuzzy and indistinct. A moment later two other chairs materialized from out of the ether waves.

Robert and his parents made their way over and they all took a seat.

Mary Anne responded to one of her son's questions. "We are doing exceedingly well, Robert. Your father and I are busy teaching classes at a school. I must say that we are most fortunate," Mary Anne looked at Marcus and smiled as she continued on explaining to her son.

"Many couples, upon their so-called death, drift into their own 'worlds'... they drift apart. Your father and I have continued working together and we share mutual goals. We enjoy being of service to other Souls who are in need or have the desire to learn and improve their state of consciousness... the two of us make a good team."

Robert listened intently before interrupting, "Mom, I cannot get over how you look. You look like you did, long ago, when I was a kid."

Marcus emphasized, "Our appearance is nothing more than a manifestation of how we view ourselves to be. Your mother's favorite memories of herself were when she was in her thirties. Mine were when I was in my forties."

"It takes a bit of practice to undo the illusions that we place on ourselves, son," Mary Anne pointed out, " I believe that if you would focus your thoughts precisely enough that you, too, could look any age that you wanted to."

"I never really thought about it," Robert responded while placing his hand on the side of his head as he reflected upon his mother's suggestion.

"Your mother is correct. These things shall unfold to you in due time," Marcus assured his son.

"The last time we saw you, Robert, was directly after you had crossed over into this dimension... you left us and traveled on to another frequency shortly thereafter. I guess you came here?" his mother surmised.

"Yes. That is correct. I have been here ever since," Robert continued, "I have longed to see you both again. I was just thinking about you and now you are here... I haven't adjusted very well to my surroundings... I am glad that you came to see me."

"Mary Anne, would you mind if Robert and I take a stroll? I would like to walk with him for a while. Are you up for a walk, son?"

"Of course, you two go ahead," she responded to Marcus.

"Yes. We can walk some if you want to, Dad." Robert said.

"I have a better idea," Marcus suggested to his wife. "All three of us can go for a walk. I would feel more comfortable to have you with us than to leave you here alone."

The look on Mary Anne's face was that of relief. Although, she wanted to give Marcus and Robert their time together, one could sense that she wanted to be with them.

"All right, Marcus. I will linger behind the two of you so that you can catch up on a few things. I would prefer to be out and about rather than to remain here inside."

"Yes, come with us," Robert concurred.

There was what appeared to be a long, craggy and coiled pathway that made its way from the perimeter of Robert's cottage toward the endless strata of mountain canyons.

Marcus and Robert led the way in their leisurely walk along the pathway. Mary Anne kept an equal pace in the rear as she keenly observed the unfamiliar landscape. She looked up at the overcast sky in search of a Sphere, or a Sun, or the pastel colors that she was accustomed to; only to find altocumulus clouds that were primarily gray in nature.

"I must say that it is quite different here in your 'world' Robert. Are you happy here?" asked Marcus.

"Not in the least bit. I am not even sure how I got here. When I first crossed over, you and mother greeted

101

me. One moment it felt like I was in your Realm and the next moment it felt as if I were falling down stairs. The next thing I knew I was here in this 'world'. It has seemed as if I have been in limbo. I spend all of my time alone. I mostly gaze out of my window as I relive my memories of when I was on Earth. It is quite depressing to be aware of all the things that I should have been doing with my life instead of merely focusing on underwriting insurance policies... I gave up on life. Somewhere along the way, in life, my priorities got turned upside down and now it seems as though I am experiencing the consequences of my behavior."

"Robert, you are summing up what I have felt all along. I sense that your 'world' is a peaceful purgatory of sort. Please do not let this world scare you. There are conditions; or states of heaven, hell and purgatory in the 'Three Dimensional Earth Plane' just as there are here in the Astral Realm. I believe that there is rhyme and reason as to why you are here in this state of condition. I can also assure you that this condition will pass. You will move beyond this situation that you are experiencing," Marcus assured his son.

"I share your thoughts, Father. I have felt so stagnated for so long. There are so many wonderful opportunities that I let slip away while on Earth."

"Hindsight is twenty-twenty," Marcus said to his son with a smile.

Meanwhile, Mary Anne noticed a small clearing in the clouds and cried out to Marcus and Robert.

"Look up there. Look at the pink and green colors in the sky," she said enthusiastically.

Marcus and Robert stopped to have a look as Mary Anne caught up to them.

"That is the first time I have noticed any color in the sky since I have been here. That is really something. It looks like a portal of some kind. 'You Light Up My Life'," Robert laughed while quoting the title to a song.

His parents expressed their amusement as the three resumed walking with Mary Anne no longer lingering behind. The three hiked along the pathway quite content with one another. It was a joy to be reunited.

Marcus walked in silence for a while, as he assessed

the current situation of his son, while Robert and Mary Anne conversed.

Marcus began to speak, "If you believe that you are ready to go forward we would like to take you back with us to our 'world'. Personally, I think that you have spent enough time here. I feel that is why I had the vision of you. I am convinced we are here to escort you to a better place where you can continue to grow through 'Spiritual Unfoldment'. You can be around other Souls who can help you. The doorway to reformation is never closed."

"Robert, you will love it. Heaven truly awaits you," Mary Anne added to her husband's proposal.

"When do we leave?" Robert smiled as he posed the question.

"The sooner the better as far as I am concerned. I want to go home," replied Mary Anne.

"May I suggest that if the time truly has come for you to leave this place that we attempt to do so now. Your mother and I shall guide you through this transition," Marcus instructed his son.

Robert appeared rejuvenated and most eager in anticipation of the endless possibilities that were flowing into his consciousness. He actually looked as if he were ten years younger as his enthusiasm continued to bubble over.

"I am ready. I am ready," Robert repeated in his excited state, "there is no reason to go back to the cottage. My 'Spiritual Suitcase' is already packed."

"**W**hy don't we settle down over there by those flattened rocks and prepare for our journey," Marcus suggested.

"Very well dear," Mary Anne responded.

"All right," said Robert.

The three made their way over and took a seat in a lotus position upon a large flattened rock. They sat in close proximity to each other so that they could join hands while forming a closely knit circle.

"We are going to guide you through this, son," Mary Anne whispered softly, "close your eyes."

Mary Anne and Marcus began chanting for some time.

"*A-u-m-m-m-m-m-m-m…*"

"*A-u-m-m-m-m-m-m-m…*"

"Robert, you may chime in if you would like," Mary Anne said.

"*A-u-m-m-m-m-m-m-m…*"

"*A-u-m-m-m-m-m-m-m…*"

"*A-u-m-m-m-m-m-m-m…*"

"Now, say the words; *I AM STILL,*" Marcus instructed.

"*I AM STILL.*"

"*I AM STILL.*"

"*I AM STILL,*" they recited in unison.

Once again, the familiar sounds and sensations overtook the couple and the next thing they knew, they were sitting on the wide stone steps above the village.

The swooshing sounds and the sensation of flying through Inner Space eventually subsided. Mary Anne and Marcus opened their eyes to find that their son was no longer with them.

"Oh my God, where is he? We have lost Robert," Mary Anne cried out.

"He did not make it. Perhaps he still has tribulations to sort out before he can ascend," Marcus pointed out.

"We have come too far to lose him again. We cannot just leave him there, can we?" Mary Anne said.

"Let's go back and try again. We shall give it another

go around," Marcus affirmed.

Meanwhile Robert, having witnessed the dematerialization of his loved ones, remained positioned on the big flattened rock. He simply sat there with a stunned and saddened look upon his disillusioned face.

Mary Anne was temporarily too disconcerted to compose herself for the state of consciousness that is required to make the return journey.

"Relax, my dear. Please, calm yourself. Take some deep, deep breaths," Marcus implored his wife.

The couple sat in a *state of stillness* for quite some time until all was calm and serene. They then made their way back to find Robert where they had left him.

Upon their arrival, Robert hugged and kissed them both. His display of affection was a sure sign of his love for them both and his strong desire to move on from his current location.

"You can do this, son, but you will need to focus more this time," Marcus said with authority.

"Visualize coming home with us. Picture those puffy, pastel colored clouds. Come home with us, Robert. Please, come home with us," Mary Anne encouraged her son.

The three sat down once again and joined hands while Mary Anne began to chant.

"*A-u-m-m-m-m-m-m-m...*"

"Breath deeply and say the words; *I AM STILL.*"

"*I AM STILL.*"

"*I AM STILL.*"

"*I AM STILL.*"

"*A-u-m-m-m-m-m-m-m...*"

"*A-u-m-m-m-m-m-m-m...*"

S-w-o-o-s-h-h-h-h-h-h-h went the sounds.

The sensation of swirling through Inner Space took a strong hold on all three Immortals this time. Robert was finally on his way home.

After the sounds and feelings of movement had dissipated the three Immortals found themselves on the big wide steps far above the mountain canyons.

"I have been on these steps before," Robert cried aloud to his father while recognizing the unique set of wide stone steps. These are the very steps that I was telling you about... the ones that I fell down when I descended to my 'world'," Robert excitedly pointed out.

"Well, take a good last look down there as you say goodbye to your old 'world'... as you leave your purgatory behind; I want you to take with you the wisdom that comes with the higher levels of consciousness... the Love for Self... Love for others... Love for the Creator of the Universe -- both inner and outer -- I want you to surrender to the Master that is within us all. I want you to shed any negative thoughts you may have. I want you to leave them on these steps and let the wind come along and blow them away for recycling," Marcus instructed his son, "Ponder on what I have said and now repeat these words aloud; *'True wisdom is becoming attuned to what I already know deep, deep down inside'.*"

Robert listened to each and every word of his father's advice. He said goodbye to the purgatory that had been his home. He quickly took a last look around at the village and endless mountain canyons that lay in the distance below him.

Robert then said the words; "True wisdom is becoming attuned to what I already know deep, deep down inside."

The enthralled family continued to venture onward.

"*A-u-m-m-m-m-m-m-m*," chanted Mary Anne, once again.

"*I AM STILL,*" Marcus avowed.

"*I AM STILL,*" Robert declared.

"*I AM STILL,*" Mary Anne affirmed.

S-w-o-o-s-h-h-h-h-h-h-h went the familiar sounds.

The mesmerizing sensations of the incredible Astral Travel had finally come to end. The three returned to their natural senses.

Robert opened his eyes to find himself, along with his parents, sitting in the meadow not far from their abode. He now looked as if he were in his mid-twenties and was full of renewed energy. His new attire resembled that of what he used to wear long ago. Robert gently fell backwards with joy, laughing, while looking up at the multi-colored sky. He then thrust his legs up and over as he executed a backward somersault before flopping back down to the ground.

Hearing the laughter and sensing that Mary Anne and Marcus were home, Shelby came running out from the meadow. The playful dog came up and licked Robert on the face as he lay on the ground deliriously pleased with his new surroundings.

All three laughed with joy at the grand display of affections that Shelby showed for the reunited member of the family. Mary Anne and Marcus had completed their adventurous journey. Their long-lost son had finally come home.

The sound of the blender instinctively sent Fluffy running into the next room to seek shelter.

"Oh come on Fluffy. Don't be such a puss, it's only a blender," Sawyer laughed while preparing his breakfast.

Sawyer, at the young age of thirty-three, had slowly become much more health conscious than when he was in his late teens and early twenties when he used to model. Back then, he was constantly feeding himself with a bag of junk food here and a bag there, in-between photo shoots. Or, better yet, no food at all, but lots of coffee.

Sawyer had developed the attitude, or mindset, that his body was the temple of his Spirit. He believed that it was important to cherish and to nurture his body, as his Soul was the Captain and his body was the Ship or the Vessel.

Sawyer's morning blender drink consisted of; an apple, a banana, eight to ten unsalted almonds, a handful of frozen strawberries, a handful of frozen blueberries, vanilla soy milk, soda water, a tablespoon of "Organic Hawaiian Spirulina" and a teaspoon of cayenne pepper.

Sawyer could see Fluffy sneak a quick look out from behind the door of the bedroom to see if the coast was clear. This had become a daily routine for Sawyer's adorable companion.

After pouring his drink, Sawyer sprinkled a hefty handful of some dry food into a bowl for his cat. The sound sent Fluffy running back into the same room that he had recently run away from.

Sawyer picked up the remote control from the kitchen bar countertop to turn on "Larry King Live" that he had taped from the night before. Larry King's guest was Rick Warren, author of "The Purpose Driven Life". Sawyer had once given Larry King a ride in his taxi and loved keeping up with the talk show host's shows.

After listening for several minutes, Sawyer processed many thoughts that were coming to his mind.

"It is great that this guy has apparently helped direct so many lost people in this world... people sure do need to discover their purpose in this life but, my goodness, gracious... he openly admits that he has tried 'going within' and 'nothing happened'... he continues to detach man from God... He actually believes that God created man, yet man is not connected to, and part of, its Creator... hasn't he read John 17:21. '...that all of them may be one, Father, just as you are in me and I am in you. May they also be in us so that the world may believe that you have sent me.' He doesn't seem to realize that 'Christ' is a consciousness or state of mind, or condition, and not an external being... of course we have a 'Purpose In Life'."

"We need to reconnect ourselves to *THE SOURCE* and realize that *THE SOURCE* is within us, as Christopher pointed out, and, it appears, Mr. Warren has not reached that stage of unfoldment in his 'purposeful life' yet. Oh well, he is doing his meaningful part in this world and I certainly will not fault the man for that... what a success story this guy is," Sawyer's mind quickly assimilated Larry's show.

"W-H-I-P-P-O-O-R-W-I-L-L... W-H-I-P-P-O-O-R-W-I-L-L... W-H-I-P-P-O-O..." went the programmed custom ring of Sawyer's telephone.

"Hello."

"Hi Sawyer, it's me, Haley."

"Haley, how have you been doing?" Sawyer asked enthusiastically, "It's been a while."

Haley is still making her living as a fashion model. This is how Haley and Sawyer met each other when they were modeling together on different job locations. They both modeled, via the same agency, for over four years.

When Haley and Sawyer first met, Haley was about twenty-one, while Sawyer was around twenty-five.

"I am fine. I have been in the Caribbean doing some photo shoots and was just thinking about you. I just got back in town a couple of hours ago. I have some time off and was wondering if you would like to get together?"

"Oh, you poor thing, the Caribbean, you say?" Sawyer joked with his friend, "Sure, I would love to."

"I may be moving back here soon," she said.

"Good to hear it. That would be nice. Listen; do you remember those Spiritual classes that I was attending when I was driving the taxi? By the way, I am no longer driving..."

"How are those going, Sawyer? The classes, I mean. Sure I remember."

"Haley, I am now teaching classes and conducting 'message readings'. My audience is growing. I am progressing so well and fulfilling goals that I never thought were possible," Sawyer explained with delight.

"That is great. I could tell that you really seemed devoted to those classes."

"I am conducting one tonight. Would you like to come check it out?"

"Well, I..."

"Oh, come on, why don't you, Haley? It might do you some good. And, besides, we can go out for a light meal afterwards and catch up with one another. Come on, won't you?"

"Sure, Okay. It sounds like fun. I am always up for something new and exciting. This has me curious, now," she said.

"Is six o'clock agreeable with you," Sawyer asked.

"That would be fine. I am staying at 'The Grand'."

"Excellent. 'Unity Church' is about half a mile from there. Do you know the place over on the Boulevard... the one with the tall Steeple?"

"Yes."

"Good, I will save you a seat up front... I will leave a ticket for you at the door under your name."

"Okay, fantastic. I am getting excited," she said.

"And please don't take it personally if I don't call your name during the session when I am conducting the 'readings'. I never know how they are going to go," Sawyer laughed.

"I am glad I called you, Sawyer. I will see you there for sure," Haley responded with a chuckle.

"See you soon, Haley."

Haley is stunning in appearance with her petite, well-built frame. Her smooth complexion is medium tan. She has long, wavy, auburn hair and big brown eyes with pretty, soft, eyebrows. Her cheekbones are high and she has a nice thin nose and voluptuous lips. She is truly picturesque.

Haley is not too religious, having been turned-off to religion at a young age. She had attended a Catholic school where some of the nuns were very impolite and lacked compassion of any kind for anyone. Some of Haley's classmates had been molested by a Priest in her school and these incidents went unreported to authorities. However, several students, including Haley, were aware of the retched offenses that had occurred long ago.

Haley strongly believes in the afterlife and had even experienced some supernatural encounters with ghosts when she was a child. She considers herself to be a Spiritual, ethical and moral individual.

"Wow, I cannot believe that Haley is coming to one of my classes. I have missed that woman," Sawyer thought to himself.

Sawyer glanced at the television, "Goodbye, Larry," he said as he shut-off the DVD and turned on some New Age Music.

AND THE DAY ROLLED ON

Sawyer's "Spiritual Reunion" class was about to begin. Since today's meeting was located in a Church, the people gathered in attendance were seated in rows, from front to back, instead of in a circle.

The lovely Haley was still not present as Sawyer introduced himself, conducted the Lord's Prayer, and began with his messages.

After a message or two, Sawyer looked toward the back of the room as the door began to open. Sure enough, in walked – better late than never – Haley.

As Haley quietly moved toward the front of the room, she smiled at Sawyer and took the special "reserved" seat that had been set aside for her.

Sawyer's stomach fluttered a bit at the sight of his old girlfriend as he returned a smile. He was very happy to see Haley and she looked breathtakingly marvelous. Sawyer drew a deep lungful of air and continued with his session.

"They are showing me a uniform. Stepping up is a male vibration. Keep in mind when I say 'stepping up' that I am not saying that in the literal sense," Sawyer clarified to the crowd.

"I think his name is Jack, or is it, Jackson... Jackson. This would be a grandfather type of vibration that may have recently crossed over," Sawyer explained.

A man in one of the middle rows raised his hand.

"Yes, sir, go ahead."

"My mother's father was Jack Lamberson. He recently crossed over..."

"Wait," Sawyer interrupted, "Did he pass away peacefully in his sleep? Was he quite old?"

"Yes, as a matter of fact he did pass on while he was sleeping. He was ninety-one," added the man in the middle row, "he used to be a streetcar driver in San Francisco and he wore a uniform."

"Well, he extends his love and he is holding up a rose as a symbol of that love. Is your mother present here today?"

"Yes, she is sitting right here." The man pointed to

his left.

"So, you are Jack's daughter then?"

"Yes," she answered nervously.

"Take a deep breath. There is no reason to be uneasy. Your father's energy is here. It is his wish to let you know that he made his transition to the other side as smoothly as one could ever imagine. And, he is quite content," Sawyer assured the daughter of the deceased man.

"Thank you."

"You are welcome. He is moving back now," Sawyer said.

After about fifteen minutes, and several messages later, Sawyer suddenly looked directly at Haley.

"Did you have a brother or somebody... someone around your age that recently crossed over from an accident?"

"Yes, my..."

"Wait, yes or no will do."

"Yes."

"I am seeing three or four energies that were... I think somebody was drinking and driving. Rick or Eric... Eric?" Sawyer looked at Haley again for a response as he nodded for her to explain.

"My brother was supposed to be in the car with his friend. His friend Eric was killed in a car crash with three other friends a week after high school graduation. My brother didn't get in the car with them because they had all been drinking. He told them not to drink and drive," Haley explained.

"Well, Eric is here. He wants to let your brother know that he is sorry that he didn't listen. He is still adjusting to his new 'world'. He is around Souls that are working with him... to help him. Are you in touch with your brother?"

"Yes, I speak to him when I call my parents. He still lives at home," Haley said.

"Please pass on the message to him that the best thing that your brother can do -- all of us can do – is to envision a white light around Eric and ask that 'Spirit' surround him with Love, guidance and direction," Sawyer explained, "Folks, you all need to be working with the Light.

Visualizations are very important. Righteousness – Right Use – is the key to the higher way of thinking," Sawyer explained to his audience.

Sawyer drew his messages to a provisional close and moved on to his teaching segment of the class.

"Let me give you an example of what I refer to as the evolutionary transition or transformation of consciousness to enlightenment when working with the Light," Sawyer said.

Sawyer turned around to face the chalkboard which was positioned behind him. The chalkboard was several feet away and rested in a wooden frame which was on wheels and was located up a few steps from the platform that Sawyer was standing on.

Sawyer asked a gentleman friend, in the front row, to be of assistance in helping bring the chalkboard down the few steps, so that it would be in better view for the audience.

Once the chalkboard was repositioned on the platform, Sawyer began to write;

1. I want to see the Light
2. I see the Light
3. I feel the Light
4. I merge with the Light
5. I and the Light are one
6. I am the Light

"You may want to write these six affirmations down and expound upon the meaning of them," Sawyer suggested to the multitude of people in the room.

Most of the audience began writing down the affirmations that were suggested while Sawyer continued to expound upon the methods of working with the light.

"First, you must have the desire to see the light. Our Creator has endowed us all..." Sawyer paused so he could joke with his audience. "...well, most of us, anyway..." you could hear the laughter throughout the room.

"Our Creator has endowed us all with the free will, to grow and to expand our consciousness, in our own way, and in our own time. This is one reason why we have incarnated into this dimension. We are here so that we can grow," Sawyer continued, "Secondly; you must use your creative imagination and visualize the light. Thirdly, after seeing the light, you must feel the light. You can do this by becoming sensitive while you imagine the brilliant, pure white light absorbing you with Love. Fourthly, after feeling the light, you must merge with the light by letting it totally envelope you. Fifthly, you must affirm that you and the light are one. Last, but not least, you must affirm that the light radiates through every cell of your body. The Light is Love. The Light is Truth. The Light emanates from *THE SOURCE*. The Light is God's *'OMNIFIC'* – which means 'All-creating' – Love, made manifest in your life, now and forever."

For the most part, the audience was very attentive and was taking notes. Suddenly a man jumped up from his seat and began quoting Scripture from the Bible.

"Hey, Teacher, Teacher; have you read 2 Corinthians 11:14. *'And no wonder, for Satan himself masquerades as an angel of light.'* Or, what about; Deuteronomy 18:10-11, have you read that?" the man continued reading from some notes that he had brought with him. "*'There shall not be found among you anyone who makes his son or his daughter pass through the fire, or one who practices witchcraft, or a soothsayer, or one who interprets omens, or a sorcerer, or one who conjures spells, or a medium, or a spiritist, or one who calls up the dead',* have you read that?" the man asked before taking his seat.

Sawyer had attended Sunday school as a child. He also was involved with Bible Study classes for a year or so and had spent countless hours watching many Evangelist Ministers on television throughout his teenage years.

"I am quite familiar with the Scriptures," Sawyer informed the man. "You have every right to your opinions but I question why you are here attempting to disrupt my service? The Bible was written by many men, spanning over a period of 1400-1500 years B.C. and then, another 100 years or more A.D., not to mention, 'God Knows' – excuse the pun – how many years beyond that, with all of the writers that were involved in further translations and formatting. The Bible isn't even presented in chronological order. Have you ever taken the time to read a version of the Scriptures in chronological order? The Book of Job is considered the oldest book of the Bible. Actually some scholars contend that it may have been written as long ago as 2100 and 1900 B.C."

The man remained silent while Sawyer continued speaking, having given the man a moment to respond to his questions.

"When 'God' apparently spoke to Moses – along with the many others that wrote down their inspirations – the information being received was, most often, pertaining to the times. Well, these times, they are a changing. And, they continue to change. I suggest that you read through '*The Third Book of Moses*', also known as '*Leviticus*'. One can clearly ascertain that many things written in the Bible no longer pertain to our times. We dress differently, we eat differently, and we live differently. Since you enjoy quoting from Scripture, why not ponder over Leviticus 1:15," Sawyer suggested.

Sawyer drew a breath after his long-winded comeback before continuing, "'*And the priest shall bring it unto the altar, and wring off his head, and burn it on the altar, and the blood thereof shall be wrung out at the side of the altar*'. In other words, Priests were sacrificing livestock by cutting off their heads and burning them. Do you advocate that we continue to sacrifice animals?"

Sawyer pressed the man, who remained silent. "Are you aware of the incest cases that are written in the Scriptures?"

"Are you familiar with the one where Abraham married his father's daughter and he still remained God's favorite? I believe it was in Genesis 20:11-12," Sawyer said as he reached for a Bible from behind the Pulpit.

Sawyer hurriedly flipped to the passage. "Yes, here it is, '*And Abraham said, 'Because I thought, surely the fear of God is not in this place; and they will kill me for my wife. But indeed she is truly my sister. She is the daughter of my father, but not the daughter of my mother; and she became my wife'*,'" Sawyer finished reciting the Scripture and then added, "I would venture to say that the consciousness of Abraham and Moses have expanded since then, wouldn't you?"

The narrow-minded man continued to sit in stone-cold silence, with his face twitching and slightly contorted, while Sawyer continued.

"On the other hand, you, simply, cannot take every word in the Bible literally, either. Goodness, gracious, with all due respect, people even thought that the world was flat back in those days. Have you ever read 'The Book of Revelation'?" Sawyer asked while flipping to the appropriate page.

The crowd remained hushed, yet attentive, as Sawyer continued to enlighten the troublemaking man.

"I believe it is chapter seven, verse one. Yes, here you go," he continued, *"After this I saw four angels standing at the four corners of the earth, holding back the four winds of the earth to prevent any wind from blowing on the land or on the sea or on any tree."*

Sawyer effortlessly continued to demand that his rude guest ponder over the "conscious-levels" of the men and women that helped write the Bible.

"While we are on 'The Book of Revelation'; the prophetic visions of John, during his exile on the island of Patmos, sparked his writings for 'The Revelation'. Wouldn't you call his visions a display of one's psychic or *'soothsayer'* abilities?" Sawyer asked.

"Jesus being transfigured upon Mount Hermon was certainly a show of 'Mediumship', was it not?" asked a fellow seated directly behind Haley.

"I would say so," Haley responded in a soft, pleasing voice.

"You will all rot in Hell!" the man yelled as he sprung to his feet and exited the premises.

Sawyer's session had totally taken a turn in a different direction from what he originally had in mind. However, the audience seemed to take pleasure in the abnormal hullabaloo.

"Unfortunately that bitter, misdirected man is blinded by his own ignorance and has missed the focal point of my classes. We can spend a lifetime arguing whether to take the Scriptures in the Bible literally or whether or not all

Scripture still applies, or ever applied, to how one should conduct his or her life. We can choose to argue, fuss and fight with one another; such as has been done for thousands of years. Or, we can grow spiritually, in individual and collective consciousness, as we expand our horizons towards good as we gain new insights into the Age of Aquarius. By the way, if any of you haven't done so already; I highly recommend that you get on the internet, if you have access to a computer, and do a search on the comparisons between Jesus and Buddha. They are truly astounding."

The audience remained silent as Sawyer spoke his mind after the commotion that had occurred.

"Before I draw this meeting to a close I would like to apologize for the unexpected outbreak. It would be nice if you all would take a moment and say a little prayer for the 'friendly' guy that just left. Send him some Light," Sawyer smiled, "On that note I bid you all a fond evening and look forward to seeing you again. There were some other things that I had wanted to go over, but quite frankly, right this minute, I have forgotten what they were. Thank you for coming, good night."

The crowd began to disassemble as Sawyer walked to the back of the room to see them off with a handshake, a smile, and a message that he vowed to deliver from his friend Christopher.

"THE SOURCE dwells deep within you."

"Thank you, good night," an elderly women hugged Sawyer farewell.

"THE SOURCE dwells deep within you," Sawyer kept repeating Christopher's words to each person as they left.

"See you soon, Sawyer, my good fellow."

"THE SOURCE dwells deep within you."

"Bless you. Thanks for your wonderful service, Sawyer."

"THE SOURCE dwells deep within you," Sawyer went on, while continuing to shake hands, as the people made their way outside.

Haley remained seated until the crowd had left the Church. The sensation of butterflies overtook her stomach.

Haley was excited to see her friend again, after such a long time. It had been almost two years since they had been in communication with one another.

As Sawyer bid his farewells to the people that were departing, Haley was reminiscing over the words that Sawyer had last said to her before they went their separate ways.

Due to their different jobs, changing lifestyles and Haley's traveling, their relationship had ultimately grown apart.

"'*Perhaps it is just timing that has turned its page to say; that we were merely passing through, yet, another day*'," Sawyer's words to Haley lay etched in her mind.

"I love that man," Haley went on thinking with a glow on her face and a smile on her lips.

"I am glad we did this," Haley said while cozily seated at a table, next to Sawyer, in a dimly lit corner of an old favorite restaurant of theirs, 'Sushi and Sake'."

"I am too, Haley. Do you remember the first time that we ate sushi together?"

"How could I forget," Haley laughed, "that was back when I still used to drink. That was the first time I tried sake. It went down so easily. I had such a hangover the next day," Haley reminisced while holding and shaking her head.

"And, it was also the first time that you ever had wasabi sauce."

"Oh my goodness, gracious, yes it was."

"I thought your eyes would never stop watering," Sawyer snickered.

"That stuff took my breath away. I thought I was going to die," Haley laughed, softly.

"We can order the 'Junmai Ginjo'. It doesn't have any alcohol in it and it taste quite good. Have you ever tried it?"

"I think that I would prefer to just have some green tea," Haley said.

"Very well, then."

"I never could figure out what to order on these menus," Haley said as she scanned her options.

"I will order for us if you would prefer," Sawyer said.

"Be my guest."

"We can start with the 'Sea Breeze Salad'. I think you will like the 'Maki' and the 'Inari' dishes. They are simple enough. And, then, for dessert, we can have some 'Strawberry-Ginger Rolls' with 'Green Tea Ice Cream'," Sawyer suggested.

"If I have room for dessert," Haley smiled while patting her stomach.

Dinner was ordered and served. Time passed by as Haley and Sawyer continued having a wonderful time catching up on what had been going on in both of their lives since they had last seen one another.

"That was a fantastic selection. You chose well, Sawyer. Everything was 'right on'. You know, this is the first time that I have ever had 'Green Tea Ice Cream'," Haley said as she marveled over their delectable dining experience, feeling totally content.

"The ice cream is rather tasty, isn't it? It is great to see you so happy... so...," Sawyer paused while tapping his fingers on the table ever so lightly, "...well, it is, just, great to see you, Haley. It truly is. I am glad that you are here," Sawyer smiled.

Haley returned the smile, "You know Sawyer; I have been making lots of money from doing my modeling. It's a strange business and there is a lot of luck involved, along with the hard work."

"I hear you on that, Haley," Sawyer concurred.

"I have been seriously considering slowing down on the modeling and either going in partners with someone, or else opening up a gallery by myself and continuing with my paintings," Haley conveyed her idea to Sawyer.

"You certainly have the talent for it, Haley. I still have the picture that you gave to me several years ago. I look at it every morning when I wake up."

"Oh, very cool," Haley responded.

She continued. "When I am modeling, I feel as though I am just a piece of meat or something... like I am an object. Everything can get so impersonal. And then, of course, everything can get so personal, with the guys flirting and all... You know how the job can get to you after a while. You have been there, Sawyer," Haley paused and put her hand on her good friend's arm.

"Everything carries its price," Sawyer said.

"When I am painting I feel as if I am really creating something. I am expressing something which is inside of me. It is as if my painting helps me to grow, or unfold, spiritually. Am I making sense, at all?"

"Sure you are, Haley. Not everyone is fortunate enough to make a living as an artist. But, you truly have a gift. Who knows what a little more devotion could lead to?" stressed Sawyer, while turning his thoughts to devoting more time to Haley.

They both sat silently and stared into one another's eyes. It was if they were reading each others minds.

In an instant, the two of them realized,

simultaneously, that their relationship may be worth another serious try as a couple.

Sawyer reached over and cupped his hand over Haley's and pressed it lightly. Then, ever so slowly, the two moved toward one another and their lips met in a long awaited kiss.

Having felt their innermost sparks ignite from the irrepressible and electrifying display of passion, one thing became obvious to both Haley and Sawyer. The two were, now, unequivocally convinced that they were more than mere friends catching up on old times.

AND TIME ROLLED ON

Sawyer turned the key, then, opened the door, to his high-rise condominium.

"Come on in, Haley. Oh, there is Fluffy. Hey 'bubba boy', meet Haley. Haley, meet Fluffy."

"What a gorgeous little cat, Sawyer."

"He still has plenty of growing to do. He is a Maine Coon Cat. They usually get pretty big, especially the males."

"Hi there, Fluffy," said Haley.

"M-e-e-a-a-h-h-h-h-h-h," cried Fluffy.

"Oh, how adorable," Haley said as she picked up her new friend, "he is too cute for words.

"He is my pal. I love Fluffy," Sawyer said.

"So what's up with this place, Sawyer? This is all new to me. How long have you been here?" Haley put down the cat and walked into the living room.

"Would you like some club soda or some tea?" Sawyer offered.

"No thanks."

Sawyer walked into the kitchen to get himself a bottle of soda water as he responded to Haley's questions.

"Well, let's just put it this way, Haley. A friend of a friend made me an offer that I just couldn't pass up. I happened to have a few dollars saved and figured that I would 'go for it'."

"I should be investing. It's just I have such a great set-up with my apartment," Haley replied.

"You will in time. There are more important things to be investing in… like what we were talking about earlier." Sawyer encouraged his friend, "Doing what makes you feel good and following your intuition. Self-expression is good for one's Soul. Your idea about spending more time painting sounds like it might be just the thing for you."

Sawyer walked over to turn on some music while the two continued their discussion. Haley made herself at home as she took a look around at the comfortable surroundings.

"Let's listen to 'Enya'. Do you still like her? This 'A Day Without Rain' CD, won her a 'Grammy' for 'Best New Age Album'," Sawyer said while turning up the volume.

"I have only heard a few songs off of that one. Yes,

'Enya' is great. Do you remember her song 'May It Be' from the movie 'Lord of the Rings'? I love that song."

"Yes."

"Her poetry is wonderful, too," Haley added as she walked into the hallway where she noticed some 'sayings' and 'writings' which were encased in frames.

DECLARATION OF PRINCIPLES

1. *We believe in Infinite Intelligence.*
2. *We believe that the phenomena of Nature, both physical and spiritual, are the expression of Infinite Intelligence.*
3. *We affirm that a correct understanding of such expression and living in accordance therewith constitute true religion.*
4. *We affirm that the existence and personal identity of the individual continue after the change called death.*
5. *We affirm that communication with the so-called dead is a fact, scientifically proven by the phenomena of Spiritualism.*
6. *We believe that the highest morality is contained in the Golden Rule: "Whatsoever ye would that others should do unto you, do ye also unto them."*
7. *We affirm the moral responsibility of individuals, and that we make our own happiness or unhappiness as we obey or disobey Nature's physical and spiritual laws.*
8. *We affirm that the doorway to reformation is never closed against any soul here or hereafter.*
9. *We affirm that the precepts of Prophecy and Healing are Divine attributes proven through Mediumship.*

"Haley, were did you go?"

Sawyer cried out from the living room.

"I am reading these affirmations on your wall. They are very inspiring," Haley yelled back as she continued reading from the interesting items that were on the wall.

"Those are the 'Declaration of Principles' of the 'National Spiritualist Association of Churches'," Sawyer explained.

Haley looked over at the simplified version of what she had just read. Only this time she read from them aloud.

"SIMPLIFIED FORM

1. **We believe in God.**
2. **We believe that God is expressed through all Nature.**
3. **True religion is living in obedience to Nature's Laws.**
4. **We never die.**
5. **Spiritualism proves that we can talk with people in the Spirit World.**
6. **Be kind, do good, and others will do likewise.**
7. **We bring unhappiness to ourselves by the errors we make and we will be happy if we obey the laws of life.**
8. **Everyday is a new beginning.**
9. **Prophecy and healing are expressions of God."**

By this time Sawyer had made his way into the hallway to join the lovely Haley. He placed his arm gently around her waist and then turned the dimmer light up just a bit to keep Haley from straining her eyes.

"These are the principles that I adhere to when I conduct my Mediumship Classes," Sawyer explained.

Haley looked over at the nine quotations that were

alongside of the other interesting writings.

QUOTATIONS

Confucianism **What you don't want done to yourself, don't do to others.**

Buddhism **Hurt not others with that which pains thyself**

Jainism **In happiness and suffering, in joy and grief, we should regard all creatures as we regard our own self, and should therefore refrain from inflicting upon others such injury as would appear undesirable to us if inflicted upon ourselves.**

Zoroastrianism **Do not unto others all that which is not well for oneself.**

Classical Paganism **May I do to others as I would that they should do unto me.**

Hinduism **Do naught to others which if done to thee would cause thee pain.**

Judaism **What is hateful to yourself, don't do to your fellow man.**

Christianity **Whatsoever ye would that men should do to you, do ye even so to them.**

Sikhism **Treat others as thou wouldst be treated thyself.**

"These are very enlightening, Sawyer. They are all saying pretty much the same thing. 'Do unto others as you would have them do unto you'. I never actually knew how widespread that 'Golden Rule' was."

"Those were also obtained from the 'N.S.A.C.'," he said.

"Interesting," Haley remarked.

"Islam also has a similar saying written in the 'Sunnah'. It goes like this; 'No one of you is a believer until he desires for his brother that which he desires for himself'."

"What is the 'Sunnah'? How do you know all of this?" Haley asked with an astonished look on her face.

"It is one of the books which form the basis of Islam. The most popular book of Islam is, of course, the 'Qur'an'," Sawyer proudly explained, "I have been reading a lot the last couple of years. I became totally absorbed with comparative Religions for a while. I wanted to find a harmonious chord... some sense of logic... whereby Religious Leaders could pool their energies and stop all the bickering amongst their selves."

"Even many of the Christians cannot see eye to eye. There are so many different sectors. It is all a big 'turnoff' as far as I am concerned," Haley expressed her dismay.

"It is rather sad if you let it get to you. But, I don't let it get to me," Sawyer shrugged while releasing his gentle hold on Haley.

"Do you ever attend their Church? This one I mean," she asked while pointing to the name of the Church that was listed in the picture frame on the wall.

"'N.S.A.C.' has locations in about thirty States. There are many Churches throughout the Country that have adopted their 'Principles'. The Church that you were at tonight, for example, is one of them. I am devoted to their 'Principles' as they apply to my beliefs with my Mediumship," Sawyer said as he began to gently caress Haley's back.

"This is all so very educational. I have learned a lot tonight and I must say that I am quite impressed, Sawyer. And, by the way, I think that you presented yourself spectacularly at the Church this evening. I was dumbfounded by your performance."

"It wasn't an act, you know," Sawyer laughed.

"No, no, I didn't mean it like that," Haley gently pushed Sawyer in fun.

Sawyer quickly and instinctively responded by reaching out and tenderly taking hold of Haley's shoulders. The happy couple, overwhelmed with emotion, wrapped their arms around one another and began to kiss, passionately.

Within a few moments, Haley's cell phone began to chime in the custom-styled sound that Haley had designated for her modeling agent.

"Oh, brother," Haley murmured in disgust.

"Who is calling?"

"It's my agent," Haley said while withdrawing from their embrace to walk back down the hall to respond to the call.

"He wouldn't be calling if it weren't important," she said.

Sawyer followed his intimate friend back into the living room as he watched her remove the phone from her handbag.

Haley read the "text message" that had just been transmitted to her mobile phone.

"HELP...IMPORTANT...TRAVEL..."

"Oh, dear..."

"What does it say," Sawyer asked.

Haley read him the message. "It says; 'Help...Important...Travel...' and, I am sorry to say that I have to call him back. This is what I was trying to say earlier... about my job and all... it is all so consuming."

Haley began dialing her agent's telephone number.

"It's ringing," she said.

"Haley. I am glad you..."

"Can't we talk about this tomorrow, Frank?" "No, no we can't, Haley. I have already taken care of your plane ticket and adjusted your hotel accommodations. We need you back here in New York, ASAP. Pamela had an emergency and had to fly home to her parents. I need you home, rested and ready to drive to Westchester before noon. This is a big account, Haley. It's a must."

"...by noon?"

"Yes, by noon. I have a ticket waiting at the Delta

130

counter. You only have one hour, Haley," her agent demanded, anxiously.

"Ah, well, all right, then. I will call you in the morning from my place after I am back in the city."

"Thanks, Haley; you're a real doll, babe."

Haley hung up and slowly put down her phone.

"He called me a 'doll'. I feel like a 'doll'," Haley uttered in a disapproving tone of voice.

"So, you have to leave town?" Sawyer double-checked, knowing that the outcome had already been surmised.

"I sure do. But I promise that I will make it up to you... to us, I mean. I don't like this anymore than you do, Sawyer."

"Let me drive you to your hotel and wait for you while you check out and then take you to the airport."

"No, I would prefer to catch an executive sedan from the hotel. Can you just call me a cab for now? It's easier this way. I can hurry faster," Haley replied as she gathered her belongings.

"You're a cab!" Sawyer joked as he picked up the phone, "Go look at your picture on my bedroom wall before you go."

"Are you referring to the one that I painted for you? Oh, all right."

Haley walked back into Sawyer's bedroom and noticed the picture. It was hanging to the left of his bed. She stared deeply into the wonderland that she had created on canvas. She turned and glanced at the rest of the room before looking back at the piece of art that she had painted for her friend. Below, on the bedside table, lay some sketches of a similar land.

"I am truly flattered that you like my picture," she said while leafing through the sketches that she had picked up.

"What did you say, Haley?" Sawyer called out from the other room. "I love that picture. I look at it every morning when I awaken."

"What are these sketches that you have here, Sawyer?"

"Oh, those..." Sawyer said while entering the room. He hesitated for a moment before explaining.

"You have heard of an 'out-of-body' experience or of 'Astral Projection', right?

"You mean an 'OBE.' Sure I have, Sawyer. I have read up on these things. I know what 'Astral Projection' is."

Sawyer walked up a little closer to Haley before briefly describing some memories of his experience.

"Well, not too long ago I had a 'doozie' of an astral journey. I took notes of my experience immediately upon my awaking. Several days later I did my best to sketch where I had been and what I had seen. I actually met the 'Medium', Mary Anne, who helps me with my 'Readings'. I met her husband, Marcus... then we were greeted by an 'Advanced-Being' that kind of reminds me of the wizard in your picture," Sawyer explained.

Haley stood there in total awe of what Sawyer was relating to her.

"Wow! Hey, listen, Sawyer, I will be back in town as soon as I can. I want to hear all about this. I also want to get back to what we were doing before my phone rang," Haley gave Sawyer a sexy smile.

Sawyer reached over and pulled Haley's body close to his.

"Me too... I wish you didn't have to go," he whispered in Haley's ear.

"W-H-I-P-P-O-O-R-W-I-L-L... W-H-I-P-P-O-O-R-W-I-L-L..."

"Your cab must be here. Let me walk you downstairs before he hits the meter," Sawyer laughed.

"Okay, love," she smiled.

"Goodbye my new friend," Haley said as she leaned down and stroked Fluffy's back from his neck to his the tail.

"P u r r r r r r r r r r r... "M-e-e-a-a-h-h-h-h-h-h," responded Fluffy with his unusual, drawn-out, meow.

"He has so many different purrs and meows. I can't keep track," Sawyer laughed.

Haley and Sawyer made their way back down the hall and toward the front door.

"I love Fluffy. He's gorgeous," Haley said.

"I guess you have to go before you can come back, ha?" Sawyer joked as he opened the door.

"I guess you do," Haley laughed as Sawyer escorted her to the cab.

Sawyer returned to his luxurious condo after having seen his good friend off in a taxicab. He could still smell the wonderful scent of Haley's exotic perfume.

"What an unexpected and marvelous day this has been," Sawyer thought to himself as he made his way into the kitchen. He grabbed a golden apple from the refrigerator along with a small bottle of soda water.

Sawyer strolled into the living room and took a seat on the sofa. He nonchalantly flipped through the television channels as his mind reminisced over his evening with Haley.

"Hey Fluffy, come here. Come over here, boy."

Fluffy sashayed over and gently plopped down on Sawyer's right foot whereby he began to purr, loudly. Cute little Fluffy alternated pressing his paws, down and then back up, the way cats tend to do.

"W-H-I-P-P-O-O-R-W-I-L-L... W-H-I-P-P-O-O-R-W-I-L-L..."

"Hello."

"Hi, it's me. I just wanted to call and let you know that today was one of the most interesting days of my life and that... that... oh, I just wanted to assure you that I will be back in town soon and maybe I can cut back on my schedule... like I was explaining, earlier."

"Are you still a cab?" Sawyer reiterated his former joke.

Haley laughed, "I am pulling up to the hotel as we speak. I am going to have to hang up now," Haley said, excitedly.

Both Haley and Sawyer were smiling and feeling like a couple of kids as they said their goodbyes once again.

"I am glad you called, even though it has only been what... ten minutes?"

Haley laughed as she said, "See you soon, Sawyer."

"See you soon, Haley."

Sawyer hung up the telephone and turned off the ringer. He then looked up at the television and quickly decided to turn that off as well.

Sawyer sat back and began to reminisce about the

first time that he had met Haley. His thoughts carried him back, almost eight years, to when they both were working for the same modeling agency.

Before they had met, Haley had been doing work for a teenage magazine, although she was twenty-one, due to her extremely young appearance.

Her first job with Sawyer was doing a unisex jean photo shoot. It had been Sawyer's designated task to lift Haley up and place her on his shoulders, whereby, in doing so, he almost dropped her.

He had, hurriedly, lifted her up and over his shoulders. However, he balanced her too far to his left and lost his footing. He came down on his left knee.

Being, limber, Haley managed to swing her right leg over Sawyer's head and slide off of him, barely holding her ground.

"What are you trying to do, send me into the next dimension? I could have broken my neck."

Haley's words echoed in Sawyer's head.

"What if I had dropped her?" Sawyer laughed, overcome with a feeling of being awkward.

"If she hadn't have been so light I would have... then, again, if she hadn't have been so light I wouldn't have been attempting to place her on my shoulders to begin with." Sawyer concluded with a smile, while recalling the incident.

"...*send her into the next dimension*... now, that is funny."

Needless to say, the two had not gotten off to the best of starts.

"Well, enough is enough. I am going to take a shower and go to bed. Fluffy, you have some dry food in your bowl and I gave you some fresh water."

After a long and relaxing shower, Sawyer walked over and looked up at the picture that Haley had painted. His eyes wandered down at his sketches of his Astral Projection.

"We truly are multi-dimensional beings," Sawyer uttered as the concept suddenly came to his mind.

He picked up one of the sketches and stared deeply as the vision of his most recent astral journey permeated his consciousness.

"To think that I was sleeping right here in this bed... yet, at the same time, I was up there... or in there... someplace or some 'place'."

Sawyer shook his head, slightly, in wonderment of it all as he got into bed and turned out the light.

"Places and things are never as far away as they seem," Sawyer thought as he closed his eyes and began to relax by taking some long and steady deep breaths of air.

An old song, composed by Johann Sebastian Bach, popped into Sawyer's consciousness as he lay, calmly, in his bed.

Row, row, row your boat,
Gently down the stream.
Merrily, merrily, merrily, merrily,
Life is but a dream.

Sawyer remained positioned on his back as he lay comfortably in his bed. He is quiescent in a "beta state" of consciousness while his brainwaves cycle at around twenty per second.

He speedily passes from "beta" to "alpha" with his brainwaves now cycling at around twelve per second. Deeper and deeper his brainwaves continue to descend.

Sawyer is now, in the "theta state" with his brainwaves cycling around seven per second.

Finally, Sawyer drifts somewhere in-between the "theta state" and the "delta state" with his brainwaves cycling as low as three to four cycles per second.

Although Sawyer had not intentionally set out to go on an astral journey, he somehow manages to do so, while in the "theta" or "delta" states of consciousness.

To Sawyer's amazement he comes to the realization that his "Astral Body" is walking on a distinctly familiar seaside.

This is the beach that he had visited when he, along with Mary Anne and Marcus, had last met with their friend Christopher of the Higher Realms.

The iridescent waves are a miraculous sight to behold as they come gently lapping the fluorescent shoreline.

There is the noticeable smell of eucalyptus that seems to suffuse the atmosphere. The curious scent envelopes Sawyer's consciousness and gives him a strong sense of wellbeing and cleanliness as he continues to saunter along the glistening shore.

"This 'place' is truly amazing," Sawyer declared to himself.

Just then he notices an Orb moving toward him from the heavens above.

"Will you look at that," Sawyer thought to himself.

At first it was impossible to discern how large of a sphere this golden-white Orb was. It could be compared to looking up at the Earth's moon when it is high in the sky.

As the Orb swiftly moved closer and closer, it appears to grow in size. It travels, swiftly, within approximately six feet from where Sawyer is now at a standstill.

By this time the luminous Orb is about three to four feet in circumference, flickering sprightly as it undulates up and down.

"Greetings, Sawyer. We meet again," sounded the Orb, as it transmutes into the shimmering figure of Christopher.

"It is nice to see you again, Christopher. Either this is one heavenly, magnificent dream or I am having another *Out-Of-Body* experience," Sawyer said.

Sawyer stood spellbound, having witnessed Christopher's transformation.

"You have indeed left your earthly body at home and paid my 'world' a visit for a second time," Christopher made it clear to his friend, "it seems as though you are becoming quite adept at this, Sawyer."

"Did you have something to do with me returning at this time, Christopher? Is there a reason for me to be here again? Please don't misunderstand me. It is wonderful to see you. I am just trying to make some sense of what is taking place."

"There is much to be unfolded unto you. This is why you were drawn here at this so-called point in 'time'. You have many questions that weigh upon your mind. Rejoice in knowing that much will be revealed to you. Shall we walk for a spell my friend?" Christopher asked graciously.

"It is so incredibly beautiful here. Surely, this must be Heaven. Yes, let's walk... let's talk..." Sawyer said, blissfully.

The two began walking alongside the seashore as Sawyer marveled over the stimulating, vibrant, colors in the atmosphere and the sensational sounds of the echoing waves.

"So, is this how you spend most your time, here, on the beach... walking, I mean?" Sawyer asked.

Christopher looked at Sawyer as he pondered over the question for a moment before answering him.

"There is continuous unfoldment from 'within', which is beyond being able to convey in words. Unlike in your 'world', where 'time' is given great importance, thoughts in this dimension tend to coalesce, or manifest, into reality much more rapidly," Christopher said as he stopped to look at the mystical sea.

Christopher glanced into the Heavenly sky as he continued, "My 'world' can be anything that I want it to be. If I seek tranquility and solitude, I can instantly transport myself to a secluded beach, such as this. If I want to experience the sound of music, *SO BE IT!*" he cried out.

"In an instant there can be the reverberation of wondrous music that consists of melodious, harmonies that are pleasing to me. When my desire is for the sublime entertainment to cease, the music subsides and there is a sense of stillness as the sounds come to an end," Christopher explained.

"You, truly, create your own reality," Sawyer remarked.

"Most definitely, indeed, I do. I spend most of 'time' beyond that of human form. If I desire to experience manifesting into a body of energy, such as you see now, I am, indeed, able to do so. If I desire to be an orb of light, in any color, I can be that, too, and can travel anywhere I so desire. You might say that I can be here, there and everywhere all at once."

"It must be wonderful to be such a 'Master' of your own reality," Sawyer said in admiration of his Celestial friend.

"Let us resume our walk," Christopher said as they continued strolling along the secluded shore.

"Even you, at this moment, are here with me and yet your physical body is back on Earth, asleep in bed. This is because we are all much more multi-dimensional and myriad-minded than you can envisage at this time. And yet, not to puzzle you, we are all One," Christopher explained in as simple words as he could.

"Do you spend much of your time as an Orb, like when I first spotted you in the sky? I still find it unfathomable of what it must be like," Sawyer asked inquisitively.

Christopher laughed, "It really is not that mind-boggling once you have experienced being in the *Higher Conscious States of Existence,*" he enlightened his friend.

Christopher continued to speak, "My consciousness is usually engrossed in an eternal state of blissfulness. I am continuously renewed by the divine energy of *THE SOURCE*, which I have told you, dwells within us all. My 'Soul Body' – I use the words 'Soul Body' and not 'Astral Body' because my 'Soul Body' is able to transcend the Astral Dimension and move on to the Mental and Causal Realms -- is renewed by unconsciously taking in a deep rhythmic cosmic breath and, then, releasing the breath in accordance with the pulsation of the universe. As I do so, I am sustained in continuous thoughts of love, contentment, admiration and devotion to *THE SOURCE*, from which I stem. The lower levels of thinking such as sickness, worry, sin or death have become less than a distant memory as they have no place here in this Realm. Their vapors dissipate way before they can ever permeate this Sphere. It is virtually impossible for discord to occur on the 'Sublime Levels of Consciousness'."

"How am I ever going to be able to remember all of this, Christopher? You have given me so much to think about."

"Simply put, Sawyer, *you will know what you need to know when you need to know it*," remarked Christopher with a warm smile.

Suddenly, Sawyer, having looked up in the sky, noticed numerous Orbs in an array of colors that varied in size.

"Look, up in sky! Look!" Sawyer shouted in excitement at the phenomenal display.

The two friends came to a halt as they watched the Orbs begin to move closer, with a lavender Orb taking the lead.

The lead Orb reached within six feet of Christopher and Sawyer. The Orb, then, began to metamorphose.

Christopher smiled at the sight of the Orbs. There were twelve of them gathered and they were all stately and magnificent.

"Give Praise -- for they are *Advanced Beings of Goodwill* -- they have come in peace. They are immersed in the Holy Spirit... they are immersed in *THE SOURCE*." Christopher assured his friend.

The lavender Orb miraculously coalesced into the image of a beautiful, majestic, indigo figure. The feminine looking entity has a lavish magenta aura which is outlined in a brilliant yellow glow that is soothing to the beholders.

Sawyer stood in amazement having watched the transformation take place.

"Relax, Sawyer, these are *Grand, Timeless*, friends of mine," Christopher informed his awestruck friend.

"Behold, my name is Trinity and I bid you a gracious good day," the 'female-like' entity announced.

The other Orbs twinkled while they remained hovering in the sky.

Trinity raised her hands to the level of her intriguing face as she sent shafts of *"Love-Light"* in Sawyer's and Christopher's direction.

They both instinctively reciprocated by doing the same in the direction of Trinity as she continued to speak to Sawyer.

"I am beyond that of 'Male' or 'Female'. Yet, I tend to show the feminine side of myself when I choose to manifest in humanlike form. Innumerable bands of *Advanced Beings of Goodwill* continually put forth considerable effort to send out harmonious thoughts of peace and love to your 'world', and to other 'worlds', I might add. We are aware of mankind's restrictions and limitations that have been collectively and individually placed upon them. With gradual unfoldment, mankind is slowly evolving and awakening to his and to her own unlimited potential. The illusions of division and separation are ever so slowly being peeled away a layer at a time to a great many Immortals as they awaken to their self-realization," Trinity revealed this enlightening information to Sawyer as the time had come for him to broaden his perception of reality.

"Everything that you say makes sense to me. It is as if I already know what you are telling me, although I had never put such thoughts into words," Sawyer said.

"Just as a newborn baby learns to crawl before it can walk; so shall mankind learn to love one another before they can experience the *'Sublime Realms'...* this is a broad-spectrum statement as the ways and means of expressing one's love for mankind can vary greatly and may also be misappropriated," Trinity conveyed.

Sawyer looked up at the remaining eleven Orbs that where shimmering in the Heavens above.

"Are they all like you, Trinity?" Sawyer asked.

"They are all unique and yet we are all the same. Yes, they are all like me," Trinity smiled as she sent out another beam of *"Love-Light"* to Sawyer.

Trinity's aura began to flicker, rapidly as she informed Sawyer that their meeting was coming to an end.

"I am glad that we had this opportunity to become acquainted," she said as she looked up at the other Orbs, twinkling.

"I will continue to channel love towards you and your loved ones back home. We are with you always. We are much closer to you than you can imagine. Behold, you are loved. Rejoice in the knowledge of it all," Trinity said as she began to transmute, once again.

Sawyer stood there, along side of Christopher, and together, they watched Trinity return to her original shape as she joined the other Orbs. The twelve Orbs, having now reassembled, swiftly ascended into the Heavens.

"That was sensational. That was truly 'out of this world'," Sawyer said in awe.

"No pun intended, right?" Christopher joked with his friend as they both laughed a little bit.

"No pun intended," Sawyer confirmed with a glowing smile.

Christopher stepped a little nearer to his friend and looked him close-up in his eyes.

Sawyer could feel an intense, yet calm, energy emanating from his Heavenly acquaintance.

"Sawyer, would you like to go on a journey with me?"

"On a journey, a journey to where?" he asked.

"Well, if you would like to, I will be happy to show you what it is like to experience traveling around the 'Interior Realms'. We can pay a visit to Mary Anne and Marcus; although we will just pass by their 'world' on your way back home. You have a 'life' to get back to on Earth. Don't forget you have a 'body' waiting for you back there in your bed. As a matter of fact, you have two bodies back there on Earth. Your friend Haley is quite a 'find'," Christopher smiled, encouragingly.

Sawyer was overwhelmed with everything that had transpired on his astral journey.

"Haley, yes she is, indeed.   I love that woman. I will have to convey my feelings to her soon," Sawyer said.

"You shall have your chance with Haley, my good friend. I would like to tell you that -- although you may not remember this when you go back into your body – you and Haley are going to be very happy together for quite some time."

"Oh really, that is wonderful," Sawyer said while glowing with excitement, "I hope that I can remember that."

Christopher smiled and said, "Like I told you a while ago, *'you will know what you need to know when you need to know it'.*"

"So, how will we get…?"

Christopher interrupted, "The same way you got here. The veil that separates your 'world' from mine, and mine from Mary Anne's, is thinner than you realize. Yet, 'inter-dimensional' travel is often, seemingly, impossible to achieve. I can easily guide you to their 'world' if you so desire."

"We will just pass by?" Sawyer asked.

Christopher could tell that Sawyer had already experienced quite enough for the time being.

"That is all," Christopher affirmed still 'shining on' with his radiant smile.

"Very well, then, take us there," Sawyer said.

Christopher began to pulsate as he raised his frequency level tenfold in order to bring about their transmutations. His golden-white aura increased in diameter as it rounded into the shape of a glowing golden-white orb.

Christopher's ever-expanding light quickly enveloped the mesmerized Sawyer and the two Immortals remarkably blended together as One as their figures transmuted into the shape of an orb.

Sawyer still had his mental faculties about him although he was no longer in a shape that he could call his own.

"We are on our way, my friend," he could hear Christopher's voice reassuring him that all was well.

"Okay," Sawyer heard his own voice respond.

In an instant, this beautiful golden-white sphere was zooming in on the Realm where Mary Anne and Marcus dwelled.

"Do you see how fast 'thought' can travel?" asked Christopher.

"This is wonderful. I simply cannot believe the miracle of it all," echoed Sawyer's bodiless voice.

"A great deal shall continue to transpire within the compounds of time and through sequences of events... ultimately; all shall lead to good and be in synchronization with the Natural Laws and the Divine Laws of the exterior/interior Universe," Christopher's thoughts reverberated deeply into Sawyer's consciousness.

"*You will know what you need to know when you need to know it,*" echoed Christopher's words once again.

"The time has come, my friend. You are homeward bound," Sawyer could hear Christopher's words coming to his mind.

"*THE SOURCE* dwells deep within you... *THE SOURCE* dwells deep within you... *THE SOURCE* dwells deep within you..." they both could hear.

Sawyer's "world" began to spin as wondrous lights zoomed in and out of focus. Sensations of Love, Warmth and Security dominated the overall remainder of Sawyer's *Out-Of-Body* experience.

Without a moment's notice, Sawyer could feel his *"Soul Body"* being snapped back into his physical body as his seven chakras realigned their selves accordingly.

Sawyer reached for a pen, then, quickly paused. He elected to refrain from doing so and, instead, placed his hand back by his side.

"I better not write anything down yet. I want to remain in this 'alpha state' for a while."

He smiled as he lay there in bed having felt a sense of being reborn after his astounding experience.

These words of wisdom came into his mind; "*THE SOURCE* dwells deep within you..."

Individuals can order a copy, or copies, of both **ANOTHER PLACE IN SPACE** and **THE SOURCE** directly @ **www.AnotherPlaceInSpace.com**.

You can also check with some online booksellers and distributors, such as **www.BuyBooksOnTheWeb.com,** or **www.Amazon.com,** or **www.Barnesandnoble.com**.

Bookstores may contact **www.BuyBooksOnTheWeb.com,** a division of **www.infinitypublishing.com** directly.

Or contact **www.ingrambook.com/new/distributors.asp** for larger quantities at lower wholesale prices which are printed by Lightning Source.